rockwell
group

CONTRIBUTORS

KURT ANDERSEN
PAOLA ANTONELLI
ARNOLD ARONSON
RAUL A. BARRENECHE
MICHAEL BIERUT
PAUL GOLDBERGER
GAEL GREENE
REED KROLOFF
TODD OLDHAM
CHEE PEARLMAN
IRWIN REDLENER, M.D.
GEORGE C. WOLFE
RICHARD SAUL WURMAN

the architecture and design of rockwell group

pleasure

First published in the United
States of America in 2002
by UNIVERSE PUBLISHING
A Division of Rizzoli
International Publications, Inc.
300 Park Avenue South
New York, NY 10010

© 2002 Universe Publishing

2002 2003 2004 2005 2006
10 9 8 7 6 5 4 3 2 1

Printed in China

Library of Congress Catalog
Control Number: 2002105953

www.rockwellgroup.com

Art Direction and Design:
Opto Design, John Klotnia,
Abby Bennett, Aoife Dorney
Contributing Art Director:
Barry Richards
Project Director: Marc Hacker
Editor: Richard Olsen
Editorial Consultant:
Chee Pearlman
Editorial Associates: Joan
MacKeith, Molly Heintz
Editorial Contributor:
Tom Vanderbilt
Design Associate: Kate Newsom
Photography Consultant:
Kevin Kwan
Editorial Coordinator:
Christopher Steighner

ILLUSTRATION CREDITS

All images are copywritten to
their original photographers,
artists, illustrators, or agencies.
The Author regrets that in some
cases it has not been possible
to trace the original copyright
holders of illustrations from
earlier publications. The Author
has made all reasonable efforts
to research the copyright holders.

Project Images
Philippe Achard: 101–102c; Max
Anton Birnkammer: 188;
Blandon Belushin: front
endpaper, 1, 10–11, 152–153 (1,
9, 26, 30, 44), 185, 141r; Shawn
Bishop: 104–105, 110, 212r (2),
214r (5); image courtesy of The
Bombay Spirits Company, USA.
Miami, FL. Photo by Shu Akashi
© CMP: 153 (48); Fred Charles:
198–199, 211–212l, 213–214l,
216–218; © Disney Enterprises,
Inc., 69, 158–159; Todd Eberle:
91l, 93r, 95lr, 153 (31); Fred
George: 146–147, 148 details;
David Joseph: 76–78, 80c–81,
82–85, 153 (40), 178–180l,
182–183; Michael Kleinburg:
52–53, 54r; Josh McHugh: 153

(32); Mary Nichols, © Disney
Enterprises, Inc.: 68, 70;
Rockwell Group: 112, 170–171
(Jamie Akers), 167t (Luis Blanc),
53 (Scott Kester), 82l (Jeff Koo),
167b (Paul Maguire), 152 (2)
(Kinnaresh Mistry), 195 (Chris
Morris), 70 (Joe Richalvsky),
153 (23) (Eric Santini), 196–197
(Tom Schaller), 153 (13) (Sam
Trimble); Jay Rosenblatt: 152
(41); Josephine Schielle: 152
(43); J. Stoll: 186–187; Timothy
Street-Porter: 170–175;
© Walt Disney World: 71r; Paul
Warchol: 20–51, 54l, 56–65,
86–90, 91r, 92–93l, 96–102l, 103r,
106–109, 116–145, 152–153 (7,
18, 22, 39, 45), 191–193,
200–207; Paul Warchol, ©
Disney Enterprises, Inc.: 160,
162, 163r–165; White Pictures:
94–95, 148l, 152–153 (4, 8, 10,
11, 17, 20, 21, 28, 29, 33–35, 38,
46); Peter Weidlein: 152 (3).

Baseline Images
Art Resource (Herbert Matter):
80l; © 2002 Barragán
Foundation, Switzerland, Artists
Rights Society (ARS), New York:
67; Bernd and Hilla Becher,
courtesy of Sonnabend Gallery:
164r; Timothy Bell: 220;
courtesy of the Biblioteca
Ambrosiana, Milan, Italy: 181r;
© Michele Burgess, Index Stock
Imagery, PictureQuest: 162;
courtesy of Deborah Butterfield
and Greg Kucera Gallery,
Seattle: 212l; © Christo, 1985,
photo by Wolfgang Volz: 180r;
courtesy of Cindy Crawford:
141r; courtesy of Cirque du
Soleil: 165l; courtesy of The
Coca-Cola Company: 189c; ©
Corbis: 28l (David Muench),
54–55 (Hulton-Deutsch
Collection), 114–115 (Mark L.
Stephenson), 143r (Todd
Gipstein), 147c (Philadelphia
Museum of Art), 154 and 180l
(Bettmann), 176l (Robert
Landau); Joseph and Robert
Cornell Foundation, VAGA: 94c;
Culver Pictures: 46, 47r, 99, 120l,
129r, 146, 150l, 163r, 165r; Do-
ho Suh, represented by
Lehmann Maupin Gallery, NY:
81; © Disney Enterprises, Inc.:
71; © Dover Publications, Inc.:
146c; Todd Eberle: 94r, 95r; Ezra
Stoller © Esto: 39r; Jose Louis
Banus-March, FPG International:
93l; GreatBuildings.com: 189l (©
Donald Corner and Jenny
Young), 214r (© Kitty Meredith);
courtesy of Hornall Anderson
Design Works: 120r; courtesy
Ken Howard: 219; courtesy I.D.
magazine: 151r; Tetsuzo Kosaka:
24r; Mark Keffer: 85r; reprinted
with special permission of King
Features Syndicate: 150r;
courtesy of Kevin Kwan: 28r,
188l; Abbé Marc-Antoine
Laugier: 25l; © Magnum Photos:
65r (Alex Webb), 139r, 140l
(Bruno Barbey); © Jeff
Mermelstein: 47l; Collection of
John C. Waddell, Photograph ©
1999 The Metropolitan Museum
of Art: 58l; courtesy of Mohegan
Sun Casino: 201lc, 202l; special
thanks to Museum Editions: 58r,
56r, 83l; Museum of the City of
New York, The Byron Collection
(cropped): 34l; courtesy of
Museum of Modern Art, New
York: 215; NASA: 109l;
Hairspray Copyright 1988, New
Line Productions, Inc. All rights

reserved. Photo by Henny
Garfunkel. Photo appears
courtesy of New Line
Productions, Inc.: 185c; John
Newsom, represented by
Silverstein Gallery, NY: 87; New
York Public Library Picture
Collection: 189r; Nobu the
Cookbook, Kodansha
International Ltd., photograph
by Fumihiko Watanabe: 22l;
courtesy of Claes Oldenburg
and Coosje van Bruggen, photo
by Attilio Maranzano: 192; Opto
Design: 194lcr; Photofest: 26–27,
38l, 40l, 56–57, 59l, 59r, 72, 86,
100–101, 127, 143l, 175, 177cr,
185r, 188c, 208–209; © Photonica:
23l, 74–75, 109c, 164l (Zefa
Zeitgeist), 32l (Christina
Alcino), 62l (T. Richards), 63r (C.
Rosenstein), 66l (Xing Pro-
ductions), 91 (Colin Samuels),
92 (Susumu Irie), 103 (Eric
Perry), 109r (Jake Wyman),
122–123 (Johner), 142 (Johner
Bildbyra), 146r (Masato Tokiwa),
163l (Makoto Takada), IBC
(NeoVision); © Phyllis Picardi,
Stock South, PictureQuest: 128r;
Pushkar © Ric Ergenbright: 141l;
Gloria Swanson Collection,
Harry Ransom Humanities
Research Center, The University
of Texas—Austin, and Gloria
Swanson, Inc., and Paramount
Pictures: 50–51; David Rockwell
Personal Collection: 35r;
Rockwell Group: 112, 181l
(Jamie Akers), 43 (Jun Aizaki),
80r (Kate Newsom), 2, 92r, 133l,
206 (Barry Richards), 102
(Vincent Celano), 6–9 (Seth
Cohen), 108 (Mike Suomi), 145
(David Rockwell), 168 (Diego
Gronda), 170–171, 218l
(Kinnaresh Mistry), 207 (Joe
Richalvsky), 6–9 (Eric Santini);
illustration courtesy of Graham
Rust, from The Secret Garden
by Frances Hodgson Burnett:
90; Stefan Sagmeister (Design:
Stefan Sagmeister and Hjalti
Karlsson, Photo: Tom Schierlitz):
139l; SIPA (Jacques Moatti):
174r; courtesy of Charles M.
Smith, © David Stiles,
www.stilesdesigns.com: 132l; ©
Luca Tettoni Photography: 33r;
J.R. Eyerman, Timepix: 156–157;
courtesy of Tootsie Roll, Inc.:
121l; Albert Vecerka: 221;
Victoria & Albert Picture Library:
132r; © Wildlife Conservation
Society headquartered at the
Bronx Zoo: 193r; courtesy of
Zion Breen & Richardson
Associates, Imlaystown, NJ: 84c.

"I always remember a dumb joke my father used to tell me," says David Rockwell, arching back in his Aeron chair, feet on desk, surrounded by the books, souvenirs, and kaleidoscopes that are his inspirations. "It's about this little kid sitting on the steps looking glum," he says. "The kid's father comes out and asks, 'What's wrong? Why are you so down?'" Rockwell flashes a grin as he winds up for the punch line: "'I'm worried because I'm afraid I'm going to flunk algebra in college.'" No matter how many times he's told this joke, it still stirs in him a smile.

In the half-dozen years I've observed the architectural escapades of Rockwell Group, I've never seen David Rockwell, no matter how frustrating the situation, respond with even a hint of discouragement—hence the resonance of his father's joke.

Rockwell's effervescence ricochets through his ninety-person studio from the top down, informing every project from its inception. The approach is not just gung-ho positivism; it's a defiant joy in bringing every possible idea to the table—and knowing there's no reason to think those ideas won't fly. My own fascination has long been with observing the creative process

in work cultures—it's what every design company wrestles with—and watching this process take place in Rockwell Group is clear proof that play, and the freedom to toss out dumb, off-the-wall ideas, are critical to the sparks that make design great.

David's personal approach to work/play is something to behold. Take, as just one example, a gala benefit he chaired for the AIDS fund-raising organization DIFFA (Rockwell contributes major amounts of time and resources to cultural and charitable causes). For this one-day event he let rip his trademark Rockwellian determination and asked a simple question of everyone he could involve, relentlessly, and over and over: Why not? Why not construct a twenty-thousand-square-foot tent next to Lincoln Center and fill it with a colossal Moroccan bazaar? Why not invite every star chef in New York to contribute their best-tasting menus to the event? Why not get Todd Oldham, Julie Taymor, Cyndi Lauper, Dale Chihuly, and other celebs to donate their talents, and at the same time, why not have Cirque du Soleil artists fly around on trapezes overhead? Then, most important, why not put his puckish, disarming, unflagging charm to work to raise nearly one million dollars for a cause Rockwell cares about deeply (his brother Rick died of AIDS in 1993)? Why not? If it can be imagined, it can be done.

Rockwell, the modern-day Prophet of Populism, has always acted strongly on his instincts, which, as many contributors to this book note, come from a powerfully formative early love of theater instilled by his mother, a vaudeville dancer. It is his finely honed sense of the spectacular and the imagining of big, unexpected possibilities that fuel him. And, as ever, a defiance of the probable: Why shouldn't a hotel lobby be transformed into a topiary garden? Why not fill a casino interior with millions of glass beads that have been woven into hanging, backlit tapestries? Why wouldn't you design a gallery exhibition with every artifact in the show suspended from the ceiling? And, when it comes to the really Big Wow, shouldn't the Academy Awards theater, home to the most watched spectacle on earth, welcome its glitterati-obsessed audience with a ten-story-high glass curtain "pulled back" to reveal the theater behind the theater of the grand arrival catwalk? Well, exactly. Why not?

David Rockwell as impresario, whether on a large, urban scale, or in a small, intimate jewel box of a wine shop like Best Cellars, is directing the mise-en-scène of experiences. Beyond the requisite conditions of a design brief, his calling is to shape emotions, adding life and human connection to what is often passed over as commodity architecture—hospitals, hotel rooms—or bringing his forte to environments

that call out for the transformative experience—restaurants, cruise ships, casinos, or even the theater experience itself. This book offers an unadulterated Rockwell Group immersion: page through and you will enter the firm's lush environments and, in the lower storyboard panel, the thinking and inspiration behind those spaces. The volume is a handbook to the Rockwellian no-holds-barred, wonder-working sensibility. That wholesale embrace of the improbable is always fearless.

Which is exactly why David Rockwell is never going to flunk algebra in college.

Chee Pearlman is a design columnist for the New York Times, *and cochair of the annual Chrysler Design Awards, which she founded for the company ten years ago. From 1993 to 2000 she was editor-in-chief of* I.D. *magazine, which was honored with five National Magazine Awards—the Oscars of the industry—under her tenure.*

7

Like primitive people who refuse to be photographed because they believe that the camera will steal their souls, creative people tend to resist the neat, reductive catchphrases that others stick on them. Robert Venturi has never much liked being called a postmodernist. And David Rockwell bridles a bit if you call him an entertainment architect.

What people usually mean by entertainment architecture is the very "duh" definition: the design of theaters, casinos, theme parks, circus facilities, stadiums, restaurants with confected back stories—venues for professional entertainment. The phrase is faintly patronizing, and Rockwell understandably resists being squeezed into the confines of the pigeonhole—of any itsy-bitsy pre-fab category.

In fact, what makes his firm's work interesting is not so much the fact that they're responsible for a lot of elaborately designed restaurants and theaters, but the fact that in *all* of the work the *approach* is that of an entertainer. To David Rockwell, the people who visit his buildings are audiences, and he is strenuously, even heroically, dedicated to keeping those thousands of customers interested, engaged, amused, jazzed, awestruck, *entertained* by the physical space itself. Entertainment is by definition populist, eager to please almost any way it can—and therefore inherently vulgar. Robert Venturi and Denise Scott-Brown notwithstanding, serious contemporary architecture mostly loathes vulgarity. Most serious architects lack the hubba-hubba gene that architects from Frank Lloyd Wright to Morris Lapidus had in spades. With the spectacular exceptions of the work of Venturi and Frank Gehry, serious contemporary architecture is very, very serious— poker-faced and cool, devoted to tastefulness above all. In an

overwhelmingly Apollonian profession, Rockwell's one of the Dionysians.

As a designer, he says he's interested in "friction . . . dissimilar things rubbing up against each other." For the last century, we've known this as the collagist's urge, of course, but I think it also constitutes a fundamentally childlike approach to design, design as a means of avoiding boredom and encouraging fun. Watch young children in their playrooms. A kid will mix radically disparate materials and textures and scales and species into a fantasy construction that has a story and makes entertaining sense to her— even if it looks motley or ridiculous to grown-ups who know that anime action figures and Lincoln Logs and chartreuse bubble wrap and Viewmaster slides and stuffed snakes and American Girl dolls don't "go" together. Young children tend more toward the baroque than the minimalist. I think most kids would sign on to the Rockwell credo: "Walls don't have to be white. Polite spaces don't interest me."

If I were going to invent a fictional childhood for David Rockwell, it would be hard to do better than the one he actually lived. His mother worked as a vaudeville dancer touring with Abbott and Costello, then as a choreographer in community theater on the Jersey Shore. When he was nine or so, he had two galvanizing cultural experiences more or less simultaneously: a day at the World's Fair in New York ("It boggled my mind") and a night on Broadway seeing his first show, *Fiddler on the Roof*. Then, a year later, his family picked up and moved to Guadalajara, Mexico—which

meant that Rockwell spent his and his generation's formative years watching bullfights and Cantinflas, essentially quarantined from U.S. pop culture as it exploded and started leeching its go-go sensibility into every nook and cranny of American life.

So a childhood fascination with theater—"the thrilling prospect," as he says, "of controlling environments and stimulating audiences"—led in college to a fascination with architecture. "Architecture looked to me like theater you could move into," he says. The impressionable yanqui boy wandering through Mexican back streets and open-air markets ("I remember cast-in-place red concrete bullrings, and light filtering through trellises") became the New York architect with an appreciation of vernacular craft, and a taste for the vivid. He went from being one kind of fish out of water in Guadalajara to a different sort of fish out of water in the architecture department at Syracuse, a latent postmodernist in a modernist temple. His heroes in college were not Mies or Corbu, but sui generis genius vulgarians—Gaudí, Maxfield Parrish, Joseph Urban—visual entertainers whose love of color and spectacle and sentiment guaranteed their exclusion from the twentieth century's canon.

And as the result of a fortuitous combination of temperament and timing, the David Rockwell approach to design caught two big zeitgeist waves.

The first wave was the one presaged by Venturi and Scott-Brown, the transformation of America into a vast, seamless mediadome. Architectural postmodernism is just one expression of a bigger paradigm shift toward the large-scale manufacture and consumption of storytelling and special effects and 24/7 *fun*. Traditional entertainment outlets have expanded madly during the last three decades—from two-screen movie theaters to six- to twelve- to twenty-screen multiplexes; from three TV channels to thirty to three hundred; from casinos only in Las Vegas to casinos all over the place. And *every* sort of built space (hotels, stores, restaurants, one's living room, one's car) became reconceived, during the 1980s and 1990s, as entertainment venues.

It's hard to imagine more fertile ground on which to build a career like Rockwell's. A cause and an effect of this shift has been a wholesale acceleration of the cultural metabolism: communication speeds up, fashion shifts more quickly, attention spans shorten, buildings are built and demolished in one generation. Under such hurly-burly conditions—more stuff competing for everyone's attention, less opportunity for any given thing to grab anyone's attention—the creation of memorable entertainment or architecture becomes more and more about creating experiential jolts, new bits of holy-cow spectacle, what Rockwell calls "wow moments."

Thus the success of his unapologetically attention-grabbing interiors, an architecture of special effects. He took Venturi and Scott-Brown's ideas and ran with them, gleefully, almost unselfconsciously, in a way that the originators have always seemed too anxious and dour to do themselves: Rockwell turned their "ducks" and "decorated sheds" inside out, making buildings that don't just entertain passersby for a few seconds, but deepen and prolong the fantasy. Casinos, for instance, are the ultimate decorated sheds, never really extending their "theming" to the interiors of the gambling halls themselves. Yet at Rockwell's Mohegan Sun casino, the half-real, half-synthetic Native American mythography is wall-to-wall, floor-to-ceiling, immersive. To use the theatrical term of art, Rockwell breaks the casino's fourth wall. He did the same thing with his sets for the Broadway production of *The Rocky Horror Show*, turning a large chunk of the stage into ersatz theater seating, thereby blurring the distinction between actors and audience in a show where that's pretty much the whole point.

His success is significantly due, I think, to his visceral comfort with (or at least cheerful resignation to) the mutability and evanescence of life. He is not paralyzed by angst about posterity and architectural immortality. "There's no way not to think about that," he says, "but I try not to let it drive the creative process, and end up producing . . . Lincoln Center. The dream of being a master builder for all time is a mind fuck." Again, the particulars of his life have inclined him to seize the moment and be here now: the peripatetic childhood, the immersion in the here-today-gone-tomorrow gestalt of theater, the early death of his father, mother, and then of his brother.

So in his work he embraces the ephemeral (colored light, LEDs, projected images) but not, crucially, the disposable. In Rockwell's highest-end work, the capital- and labor-intensive craft (millions of woven beads and a sixty-foot-high alabaster mountain at the Mohegan Sun casino) mitigate the pop insubstantiality. The buildings may be stage sets, but they're awesome stage sets that will last as long as they need to last.

The second wave Rockwell caught is the generational shift toward Peter Pan–ishness. As a matter of style and etiquette, adults today no longer regard adulthood as a fundamentally distinct zone from childhood; people born since World War II are driven by a pursuit of instant gratification and informality that used to be the exclusive province of children and teenagers. When I was young, parents did not wear blue jeans and sneakers, take bike rides, listen to rock-and-roll, watch cartoons on TV, buy comic books, play video games, go to science-fiction movies and theme parks without children, cultivate connoisseurship of cookies and ice cream, or, when talking to friends about their jobs, ask, "Are you having fun?" Today they do.

Today people work and eat and shop and live in playhouses. And so David Rockwell—a forty-five-year-old man in sneakers and long hair who collects kaleidoscopes—designs buildings intended to please middle-aged children. Rockwell has called his Pod restaurant in Philadelphia "a big jungle gym." For adults, the pleasures of Cirque du Soleil (and Rockwell's theaters for Cirque) are the childlike wonder they induce. The twenty-five-foot-high baseball cards at Turner Field in Atlanta, the cartoony Hollywood lobbies for Loews 42nd Street, and Animator's Palate restaurant on the Disney cruise ships *Disney Magic* and *Disney Wonder* are all theatrical in a theme park sense, with kiddie-esque special effects intended in each case primarily for adults.

Speaking of Disney, David Rockwell is obviously not the first American to make his name and fortune dreaming up recombinant entertainment experiences that mix storytelling and architecture and special effects. Indeed, he is working in an even older tradition, which Walt Disney revived and refined—that of P. T. Barnum, who put up grand, over-the-top buildings to house his extravaganzas, and whose genius was ignoring the conventional boundaries between theaters and museums and circuses, between entertainment and education, public and private, high and low, fantasy and reality.

And it's important to remember that fantasy feeds and shapes reality. As Disneyland helped inspire a generation of earnest architects and planners to invent New Urbanism, so have Rockwell's never-never-land casinos in Connecticut inspired the Mohegans to reimagine and reanimate their own tribal culture. And so the phrase "entertainment architecture" doesn't quite do the work justice. Particularly given his wonder years in Mexico, a more apt pigeonhole might be a literary one from Latin America: David Rockwell, architecture's turn-of-the-twenty-first-century magical realist.

Kurt Andersen is author of the critically acclaimed best-seller Turn of the Century, *and the host of* Studio 360, *a weekly program about culture broadcast nationally on public radio. Prior to cofounding* Spy *and* Inside.com, *Andersen was editor-in-chief of* New York *magazine, a columnist for* The New Yorker, *and the architecture critic for* Time.

Many of Rockwell Group's projects, particularly their restaurants, are often described in terms of theater, or sometimes film. To some degree the theatrical label is inspired by interiors whose colors, light, textures, eclectic "props," and ground plans seem more like stage settings than interior design. But ultimately the theatricality refers to an emotionalism and narrative quality that had been largely eradicated from the twentieth-century architectural vocabulary by modernist aesthetics.

David Rockwell welcomes the association with theater because to him it implies "emotion, narrative, the ability to tell stories—that which can profoundly move you." These are the elements he wishes to bring to his architectural endeavors. Rockwell's early influences were, in fact, from the theater; he cites productions of *Fiddler on the Roof* and *Cabaret* as formative experiences. But what he gleaned from these performances was the way in which the scenic elements, particularly the movement of light and the shifting of sets, manipulated the emotions of the spectators and the dynamics of the shows. His fascination with the stage was such that he took a semester off from his architectural studies to work with lighting designer and theater consultant Roger Morgan.

It is therefore not surprising that many of the architectural influences Rockwell acknowledges tend to come from the Italian Renaissance and Baroque eras, particularly works by Michelangelo and Borromini. These artists, especially in their churches, piazzas, and public sculptures, drew people (read audiences) into each space and carefully led them through an unfolding narrative, all the while delivering the dramatic qualities of surprise, astonishment, and awe. Among the specific works Rockwell cites, one in particular stands out: Michelangelo's mannerist design of the anteroom of the Laurentian Library in Florence. In this enclosed vestibule Michelangelo disrupted the prevailing neoclassical tenets, and in the process created an entryway that would become more famous and significant than the library itself. The pediment over the main door is broken; pilasters taper unexpectedly toward the ground; structural columns are recessed into the walls, seemingly negating their function; the staircase itself ("nightmarish," says art historian H. W. Janson) seems to flow lava-like downward from the doorway, almost defying anyone to ascend; and of course there are the haunting blank niches whose dark frames draw attention to their emptiness. Almost every element of the room seems to defy logic and expectations. In other words, here is an architectural space totally irrelevant to the purpose of the building (a library) that nonetheless has a profound emotional effect upon anyone entering the space. Within this enclosure, form and function are completely subverted to an expressive— that is to say, theatrical—vocabulary. Michelangelo created a terrifying stage space, a kind of architectural drama of transition, through which patrons of the collection must pass as they move from the public world of the city to the private world of the Medici books and manuscripts. While Rockwell Group may not aim for such disconcerting emotions in their architecture (restaurants, hotels, and ballparks do not want to evoke terror), David Rockwell nonetheless seeks an equally profound impact upon those who move through the spaces of his office designs. "I'm not interested in static, monumental architecture," he explains. "What interests me are transitions." To achieve their goals, Rockwell Group's work draws upon the emblematic, iconographic, and environmental vocabulary of stage settings as well as the radical, often startling juxtapositions and rhythms of contemporary media.

On a certain level, architecture and theater design are fundamentally the same. They both involve the trans-formation of space, the control of movement through that space, and— through the use of color, line, texture, volume, and iconography—the communication of information while manipulating the emotional response of spectator-occupants. In the *Poetics,* the ancient treatise on tragedy, Aristotle employs the term *skenographia* (scenography)—scenic writing—to refer to the visual aspect of theatrical production. While scholars still debate what, specifically, Aristotle may have meant by this word—since there was almost certainly no use of the illusionistic or play-specific scenery we now associate with theater—the term nonetheless has a particular resonance today. Ours is an increasingly visually oriented society and the visual is something to be read, to be interpreted, just as literature and language were in the past. In the case of theater, the spatio-imagistic or scenographic world of the play provides a narrative that is equivalent to that of the dramatic text. Similarly, once the architect's work moves beyond the merely functional and into the world of the symbolic and emblematic in which the visual and spatial aspects are intended to convey ideas and create emotion, it, too, is a form of *skenographia.* Architects are inscribing a text—a dramatic text or narrative—upon the landscape. Any architectural creation, from a room to a building to a cityscape, tells a story through sign and symbol; it shapes the movement of the "characters" within the environment through definition of space and thus defines relationships among these characters.

The arts of stage design and architecture have always been intertwined. In some of the most productive periods of theater history—classical Greece and Rome, ancient India (Sanskrit theater), medieval Japan (Noh), and Elizabethan England, for example—design and architecture were one and the same; the permanent architectural features of the stage and theater building served as the scenic environment, and there was little or no separately created scenery. When stage design emerged as an art—indeed, as a profession—in the Italian Renaissance, most of the stage designers were, first and foremost, architects. Architecture, after all, was intended to provide a symbolic and emblematic space in which the business of state, church, or domestic life could unfold. Similarly, the designer of a stage setting was creating an ensemble of visual images that would convey the symbolic and metaphoric aspects of a fictional story through means which were intended to inspire wonder, awe, and delight.

One of the first scenographers was the fifteenth- and sixteenth-century architect Sebastiano Serlio, who created plans for some of the first modern theater buildings and devised three standard stage settings that were intended to serve all genres of drama. Using forced perspective painting—a relatively new technology at the time—on angled wings known as flats, he created an urban setting of formal buildings for tragedy, an urban setting of shops, taverns, and bourgeois houses for comedy, and a bucolic setting for satyric plays or pastorals. In other words, Serlio created a total architectural environment or landscape, and presented it through scenographic means on the stage as a background for dramatic action. Among the most stunning theatrical creations of the Renaissance and Baroque eras were the court festivals of the Medici, the Hapsburgs, and those of Louis XIV at Versailles. Often staged as parts of larger celebrations of weddings, coronations, birthdays, and the like, these performances were mostly allegorical spectacles in which the dramatic text played an almost secondary role. Therefore, the designer was, for all intents and

13

purposes, the playwright as well. The architect-scenographer created both the packaging and the content, as it were: the stage and the spectacle. The stage, in the most elaborate cases, involved the creation of gardens, fountains, and buildings—thereby blending aspects of scenography with elements of landscape architecture, structural engineering, and even urban planning to create the Baroque equivalent of multimedia spectacles. Spectacle and architecture seemed to merge. By the eighteenth century such architectural-scenic spectacles had largely disappeared, along with the absolute monarchs, but the process, in a sense, would be reversed. Cities and parks began to be conceived as theater; architects would transform both nature and metropolis into virtual stages—in real time and space—for the unfolding of human dramas. Think of the gardens of Versailles or Kew Gardens in England or the urban plans of Pierre-Charles L'Enfant for Washington, D.C., Karl Friedrich Schinkel's designs for Berlin (Schinkel was also a significant scenographer and architect of theater buildings), Baron Haussmann's redesign of Paris, or the creation of the Ringstrasse in Vienna. All of these schemes were intended to effect total control over a vast urban or natural landscape—just as a director controls the space of the stage—creating a symbolic and emblematic environment that would determine the movements of the "players" within the space, while simultaneously telling a story about that particular society.

Despite this long and respectable association of theater and architecture, the modernist architectural dictum of "form follows function" allowed no room for the implicit superficiality of theater. Thus, through much of the twentieth century one of the most negative epithets a critic could hurl at a work of architecture was to deride it as "theatrical." This was the charge, for instance, leveled against the early-twentieth-century scenic designer and architect Joseph Urban—an acknowledged inspiration for David Rockwell. Following his success as a designer and architect in Europe, the Viennese-born Urban came to the United States in 1912 as a designer for the Boston Opera and went on to a prolific career in this country as stage designer for the seemingly antithetical arenas of the *Ziegfeld Follies* and the Metropolitan Opera as well as the films of William Randolph Hearst. Urban also continued his architectural pursuits, primarily with hotels, department stores, restaurants, and private homes. Among Urban's architectural projects were two landmark New York City buildings: Hearst's International Magazine Building (1929) and the New School for Social Research (1931). The former was labeled "theatric architecture" by *The New Yorker*; in the latter, according to critic Edmund Wilson, Urban's attempt "to produce a

functional lecture building [resulted in] a set of fancy Ziegfeld settings which charmingly mimic offices and factories where we keep expecting to see pretty girls in blue, yellow and cinnamon dresses to match the gaiety of the ceilings and walls." In the 1950s, the exuberant Miami Beach hotels of Morris Lapidus suffered a similar fate at the hands of critics; their gaudy populism flew in the face of officially sanctioned high-culture architecture. These and other similar approaches to architecture seemed to evoke the most negative connotations of theater.

In contemporary Western society in particular, theater is more often associated with entertainment than with the civic, social, and religious roles it has occupied in other cultures or periods. It is thus seen as nonessential, as frivolous, as self-indulgent; it is redolent of excess and flamboyance. In short, theater is classed with popular rather than serious culture, and in the modern era, the popular—except perhaps as something to be quoted by the avant-garde—was suspect. Moreover, theater tends toward self-referentiality ("all the world's a stage," wrote Shakespeare). But as minimalist and essentialist modernism came to dominate the arts of the early twentieth century, as functionalism replaced aestheticism, anything decorative (i.e., nonfunctional) was to be avoided. The decorative element was, in fact, the primary issue with Urban's creations. The champions of the increasingly dominant International Style saw the International Magazine Building as a pastiche of classical references. And while the New School for Social Research mimicked and exploited the International Style, Urban could not resist incorporating decorative elements within the design. Urban was making artistic decisions based upon a visual aesthetic that had little to do with the particular and necessary usage of the structure. In the late nineteen-twenties, such an approach to architecture was anathema.

Finally, theatricality also suggests a lack of stability. Theater, after all, is an ephemeral art that evaporates into thin air with the final curtain, leaving behind only fragmentary traces. Architecture, on the other hand, embodies a certain sense of permanence, even a hint of eternity. To label a work of architecture as

theatrical is to imply that it is impermanent, even disposable, which seems to fly in the face of accepted wisdom. (It is perhaps worth noting that the ancient Greeks, whose architecture is living proof of the enduring potential of architecture, also created drama, which despite its incorporeality, is still performed 2,500 years later.)

But the antitheatrical prejudice of modernist architecture has been giving way in recent times to a new theatricalism. Whether in the museums, office buildings, and homes designed by such architects as Frank Gehry or Rem Koolhaas, or in the restaurants, hotels, and entertainment complexes of Rockwell Group, theatricality has come to be not merely acceptable but almost the dominant form—the new lingua franca of architecture. Ironically, this return to the theatrical comes at a time when traditional theater itself has lost much of its cultural importance within contemporary society. Despite the attenuation of theater as a locus for moral debate, social investigation, and simple storytelling, the culture as a whole has become increasingly theatricalized thanks largely to the impact of electronic and visual media. The reference points of the contemporary world are television, film, video, computer graphics, and various permutations of rock/pop music and their related venues (stadium concerts, clubs, MTV, personal stereos, the Internet, etc.). Rapid movement, intense color and light, continuous visual stimulation, and high-decibel sound make up the palette from which this new architecture is drawn. We are in a world of sudden and jarring transitions that often result in bold and unexpected juxtapositions and contrasts. The impact of media has had an obvious effect on traditional theater itself—plays with linear narratives and an emphasis on dialogue over physical action appeal to a rapidly diminishing audience. Most dramas now employ more lighting instruments than the standard musical of, say, thirty years ago because audiences' threshold of acceptable visibility has increased; almost all professional productions are now acoustically enhanced or amplified; standard narratives have largely given way to associative and juxtapositional images more closely associated with the hypertextual world of cyberspace than with classic storytelling. Similarly, in the realm of restaurant and hotel design and experience, such virtues as simplicity, elegance, and even romance are evaporating and being replaced with the idea of event or performance.

If a room, a restaurant, or a ballpark is understood as a kind of performance, then it must, on some level, be designed as a stage set. The Czech semiotician Jiri Veltrusky, in a 1940 essay, made the crucial insight that everything on the stage is a sign; any object, however mundane, is transmuted into a charged signifier by the power of the stage frame. Rockwell Group uses architectural space as a stage-like frame and places within it a range of related symbols whose total effect may be greater than their individual meanings. The Japanese restaurant Nobu in New York City, for example, includes birch trunks (that enclose lights) out of which spread squared wooden poles that simultaneously suggest stylized branches as well as structural supports for the ceiling. Birch branches also form screens for private dining alcoves; stylized chopsticks form the legs of the bar stools; cherry blossoms are stenciled onto the wood floor; one wall is covered with embedded river stones. The sushi bar was conceived as a metaphoric stage set within the context of the restaurant, and the mosaic wall behind it serves to bring the sushi chefs into dramatic relief. While the overall effect evokes the Japanese countryside, it is not a simulacrum (not a realistic set, to use theater terms) but a suggestive collage. The Mohegan Sun casino in Connecticut was similarly approached. Though evocative of Adirondack hunting lodges and Native American villages, the casino is more of a thematic environment of icons and emblems drawn from Mohegan culture and history interwoven into a multifaceted entertainment complex. Visitors to the casino and its restaurants are entering into a forest of symbols (to borrow Baudelaire's phrase). But the theatrical framing creates a gestalt that allows the spectator to meld the images into a coherent whole.

David Rockwell, like the artists of the Wiener Werkstätte, Joseph Urban, and Frank Lloyd Wright before him, understands the need to design all the elements contained within a given space. Rockwell Group designs or supervises the furniture, wallpaper, decor, and all the elements that make up the visual and spatial environment. It is an architectural equivalent of the Wagnerian *gesamtkunstwerk*—the total artwork in which a single visionary artist controls all the component performative elements within the ensemble. In this regard, Rockwell Group's spaces are clearly analogous to stage settings; Rockwell Group embraces theatricality, and each of their projects can be seen as a performance or self-contained drama. In every one of their projects there is an implied spectator. The spaces are designed to engage the viewers from the moment they enter into the space (or first have visual contact with the structure), to their passage and movement through the space, to their interaction with the total environment. Rockwell Group is interested in particular effects that are normally associated with theater: the initial impact through revelation of space, seduction through the combination of visual iconography and spatial manipulation, and emotional transition or transformation.

Every performance has an "entrance," that is, a moment and place where the activity and rhythm of the quotidian world ends and the fictive or festive world of the theater begins. Traditionally this event has been marked by the revelatory opening of the front curtain, through a change in lighting, or it has simply a vocal, musical, or percussive "announcement" that the show is about to begin. For Rockwell Group, entrance, which implies transition, is one of the most powerful aspects of theater. Perhaps this is why the entrance to the Laurentian Library is so appealing to them. In a sense, the grand entrance also harks back to the opera houses of the nineteenth century, which extended the concept of transition and transformation to the theater building itself. Nowhere is this sense of celebratory entrance more evident than at the Paris Opéra ("one of the great theatrical spaces," says David Rockwell), whose foyer and grand staircase announce a spectacular transformation from the prosaic to the dramatic and envelop spectators as it almost literally sweeps them into the dazzling world of the theater.

Because theater implies a dichotomous relationship between spectator and stage—generally there is a static viewer observing the action that unfolds within a carefully delineated space—transitions occur in front of the spectator through the movement of scenery, light, and the performers themselves. Although architecture sometimes creates passive spectators as with facades that advertise the function and content of a building or the grandeur of certain interior spaces meant to inspire awe, more often it creates an environment in which the spectator and performer are one and the same. The "spectator" in a work of architecture generally does not observe the work from outside the frame but occupies the designed space—the stage, as it were. Transitions in architecture are generally achieved by movement of the performer-spectator through the space. (Of course, in many folk, festival, and religious performances throughout the world, as well as various performative and paratheatrical activities—parades, sporting events, political rallies, etc.— boundaries between performer and spectator dissolve, as do distinctions between performance and spectator space. In such paratheatrical events, as in architecture, linearity or sequentiality is often replaced by simultaneity.)

Nowhere is this more evident than in the Kodak Theatre. As the new home for the Academy Awards, this space that celebrates transition was recently seen by several hundred million people. The Oscars, in many respects, are remarkably like the late medieval performative event known as the royal entry. On these occasions, a monarch and his or her entourage would enter into a town with great pomp and be received by the populace with scenic spectacle and performative activities. A key element in these events was the phenomenon of the dual spectator/dual performer. The nobility functioned both as prime performers but also as prime spectators, while the residents of the town also functioned in both capacities. At the Oscars, the Hollywood celebrities function in the role of nobility; they are at once the show and the audience, arriving to be seen, but also to observe. The Kodak Theatre must provide at least two transitional spaces—from exterior to interior and from auditorium to stage. The exterior serves as an arrival stage. The "nobility" disembark, pose for the assembled spectators (both physically and electronically present) and then move from the public space of the street into the private space of the theater. Here Rockwell has provided an extra transition, important for the participants but mostly invisible to the television audience: a grand staircase, reminiscent of both early-twentieth-century movie palaces as well as the Paris Opéra, that sweeps the audience from the public space of the street to the mediated public space of the auditorium. Once inside the auditorium there is a less well-defined transition space from the seats to the stage. Normally, the only transgression of the invisible stage wall is through the senses of sight and sound, but on Oscar night, at least, certain spectators await with great anticipation the opportunity to move from the seats to the stage, a transition that is re-inscribed by the camera for the audience that exists beyond the walls of the theater. Because the official audience inside the theater is also the object of viewing for the television audience, the interior of the theater must also function as scenic decor. Rockwell has created a giant "mouth" of a proscenium evocative of Radio City Music Hall and the greatest of old movie palaces (and a plush color scheme also evocative of that era), but included tiers of boxes along the side walls that evoke eighteenth-century opera houses (albeit with a more modernist line). In place of a solid dome over the auditorium is an open latticework of arches and ovals, some patterns inspired by Busby Berkeley choreography, that, at least on Oscar night, provided an aerial stage for Cirque du Soleil. The arches spanning the auditorium reflected the shape of the proscenium so that the auditorium viewed from the stage—as is frequent in the televised performance—becomes a reverse stage with spectators as performers. Thus, not only does the theater mediate between interior and exterior, but between live and televised, between stage and auditorium, between floor and ceiling. It is a space in constant transition in which the separation of performer and spectator space is fluid.

Stairs are obvious representations of transition; they transcend space, allow vertical movement, and connect disparate locales. Their shape dictates the flow of vision and the movement of bodies. Together with doors they are the oldest scenographic elements, having existed on the classic Greek stage by the middle of the fifth century B.C.E. Not surprisingly, stairs form an integral part of Rockwell Group's vocabulary. In the W hotel on New York's Union Square the curving staircase—reminiscent of the one in the film *Sunset Boulevard*—dominates the relatively narrow lobby as it sweeps from the upper ballroom, transforming the otherwise unassuming space into a piece of heightened drama. Along with transition, another appealing aspect of theater for Rockwell Group is the element of surprise; each opening of the curtain or each change of scene brings the unexpected. The surprising element in the W Union Square lobby is not the staircase per se, but a rectangular patch of wheatgrass at the edge of each step. It is a touch of postmodern hyperrealism—incorporating natural elements within a constructed, artificial world. The juxtaposition of the organic and artificial, a common scenographic ploy in much contemporary stage design, creates jarring contrasts that call into question ideas of reality and illusion. Just as everything on a stage, by virtue of being framed, is a sign—a kind of

quotation from the world outside the frame—so too the elements in Rockwell Group's designs are quotations of a sort. The patches of grass refer, on some level, to Union Square Park across the street, but amid the concrete and glass of New York City, parks themselves are a kind of stage or frame in which nature is quoted.

Other grand staircases can be found in Rockwell Group's restaurants Rosa Mexicano and Ruby Foo's (whose staircase evoked images of *Auntie Mame* for former *New York Times* food critic Ruth Reichl). Both ascend past what can only be described as scenic backdrops. In Rosa Mexicano the stairs climb past a blue tile wall on which are mounted hundreds of plaster statuettes of divers and over which water gently cascades (a postmodern tribute to Busby Berkeley, perhaps?); in Ruby Foo's the staircase ascends along a wall of oversized red lacquer boxes containing a pastiche of Asian icons and images. The staircases are focal points of the restaurants, and anyone on the stairs automatically becomes a performer silhouetted against a decorative, theatrical background. At the same time, the stairways provide a vantage point for spectators to view the drama of dining above and below. The patron on the stair is both performer and spectator, just as the diners at the tables can function in both capacities.

Illusion, of course, is a key element in much theater design and it, too, plays a role in Rockwell Group's creations. For the Walt Disney World home of Cirque du Soleil, Rockwell Group created what appears to be an idealized circus tent. In reality, the main housing is a solid structure containing stage and auditorium, but a tentlike "skirt" is stretched around the building, anchored by steel cables, and a "crown" tops the structure—all evocative of the grand three-ring tents of Ringling Bros. and Barnum & Bailey, especially at night when dramatically placed light glows through the "tent" and picks out the distinctive curves of the crown. It doesn't matter that the interior has nothing to do with a tent (patrons are probably just as happy not to have to sit on uncomfortable wooden bleachers); the audience has been given the illusion of entering a tent that is still the symbol most closely identified with the circus. Illusion also plays a part in the Rockwell Group–designed dining room of the Disney Cruise Lines ships *Disney Magic* and *Disney Wonder*. The walls

of the cruise ships' dining rooms are covered with black-and-white drawings of Disney cartoon characters. During the course of the meal, the images transform into full color. The gradual transition is almost imperceptible and calls into question the reliability of perception. (It may also, in a most ironic way, echo the scene in Michelangelo Antonioni's film *Red Desert* in which, as the camera pans a room in a continuous circular motion, the colors of the walls of the room are different each time.)

Over the past three centuries or so, theater has come to be associated with a particular form of literary art— the play. But historically, theater has encompassed a wide range of spectacle and entertainment in which conventional drama makes up only a small percentage of the whole. The study of Renaissance theater, for instance, tends to focus more on tournaments, royal entries, aquatic spectacles, fireworks, and royal wedding festivals than on drama per se. Such events often blurred distinctions between performer and spectator, performance space and audience space. Similarly, when the history of contemporary theater is studied in the future, it will no doubt encompass sporting events, rock concerts, discos, fashion shows, parades and fireworks, and perhaps even shopping malls. Entertainment architecture can thus be seen in the larger context of performance.

One of the historical functions of theater has been to reinforce the social structure by helping to inscribe history as well as contemporary moral and aesthetic codes on the civic consciousness. Just as Renaissance spectacles were better suited to that role in their time than the conventional drama, so too today that function is fulfilled more by electronic media and entertainment than by traditional theater forms and institutions. But this shift from theater to electronic media has resulted in a concurrent shift of focus or emphasis from the content to the structure. All societies have liminal spaces: locales that provide a transition from one segment of society or one part of the cityscape to another; places where the standard rules and behavior do not apply because they exist outside the spatial or temporal boundaries of official

society. But in the postmodern world of cyberspace and instant communication and even the banality of channel surfing, it is the transition itself that has come to dominate. Continuous transformation has become the norm and content has become the liminal. Rockwell Group's architecture, aside from emphasizing the centrality of entertainment as an almost religious force within our society, places a premium on the structures of transition.

An admirer of Joseph Urban once observed that it was theoretically possible to travel from an Urban-designed home in an Urban-designed car to a restaurant, then theater, and finally hotel—all designed by Urban. Rockwell Group has yet to design an automobile, but it is otherwise theoretically possible to journey similarly amidst an entertainment and domestic world of Rockwell Group's design. But whereas Urban's structures and designs tended toward the monumental, Rockwell Group tends toward creations that are at once as transitory and pervasive as the electronic media images of current society.

Arnold Aronson is a professor of theater at Columbia University and writes frequently about theater design and architecture. He is author of American Set Design, The History and Theory of Environmental Scenography, American Avant-Garde Theatre: A History, *and* Architecture of Dreams: The Theatrical Vision of Joseph Urban

15

educe

It might seem that the emblematic experience of a Rockwell Group design is to be had by burrowing deep into one of the many worlds Rockwell Group has made themselves—in the Asian stage sets of restaurants Vong and Nobu, say, or the panache of the Academy Awards auditorium, or the sleek sheen of the first W hotel, W New York. Total design is, after all, Rockwell Group's mantra, and in their best work they manage to craft not just a physical setting but an emotional moment so all-encompassing that everything that they did not design recedes into invisibility.

But the most revealing place Rockwell Group has designed is not one of these self-contained environments, gloriously entertaining though they are, but a pair of alcoves in the lobby of their Chambers hotel on West Fifty-sixth Street in New York, which seem at first to be the exact opposite of the rest of their work. Each alcove contains a few voluptuous pieces of furniture, which are placed beside panels of glass running all the way down to the floor. The glass faces the street, and if you sit in one of these alcoves, the energy of the city seems to rush toward you. The panels feel less like windows than like huge screens on which a film of street life is constantly projected, and you are not sure whether you are sitting on the sidewalk being part of it or sitting inside looking out at it. Ambiguity—which is subtly implied in all of Rockwell Group's work in the way it is subtly part of any stage set—here breaks free, and becomes a powerful force of its own.

By connecting you to the street, however, Rockwell Group has done something else with the Chambers lobby, which is to reveal in literal form what all of the rest of their work implies: the power and the presence of New York. The city's intensity, its wild mix of cultures, its constantly shifting visual stimuli, its smorgasbord of historical styles—all of these are influences in Rockwell Group's work, which almost always embodies New York's cosmopolitanism even as it rarely takes the city as a direct subject.

Rockwell Group makes sophisticated versions of fantasy environments. Or is it fantasy versions of sophisticated environments? Either way, what they do is more or less what the city itself has always done. Rockwell Group's architecture is a kind of metaphor for New York. It is a collage, brimming over with energy, and yet composed with far more order and coherence than it seems to possess at first glance. New York is itself a sequence of stage sets, of fantastic architecture tamed (or exaggerated) to satisfy the needs of commerce. You could say the same of Rockwell Group's oeuvre. It is fantasy made practical so it will make money, and kept exuberant so it will entice the crowds. Rockwell Group understands this balance better than anyone else in the business. They also understand the basics of proportion,

scale, movement, and light. They understand image, I think, best of all. They know exactly how strong to make it. Rockwell Group hasn't invented a new architectural language, but they seem to have a kind of perfect pitch for picking up on the essences of those architectural languages that other people have used before, and making them feel exactly right. If that isn't a New York quality, then nothing is.

Rockwell Group's work is based on a principle that New York as a city has always followed: that cities are venues for entertainment as much as for commerce and that these two functions are inextricably intertwined. They have gone together throughout urban history, but now they seem more interdependent than ever, since no one can pretend any longer that the city is necessary for doing business in the way it once was, and its future as a place of entertainment becomes ever more apparent. To Rockwell Group the very notion of public space involves entertainment: so does the idea of the street, the square, and the restaurant and the hotel. The distinction between private and public space in Rockwell Group's world is not particularly strong, largely because they make private

spaces that are intended to function as public ones; given how the line between private and public space has all but disappeared in cities today, it is fair to consider Rockwell Group and architects like them to be the equivalent of the urban planners of another era. They make what public space we have.

Paul Goldberger is the architecture critic for The New Yorker. *Formerly the architecture critic for the* New York Times, *where he won a Pulitzer Prize in 1984 for his criticism, he is also a contributing writer at* Architectural Digest *and the author of several books, including the text for* The World Trade Center Remembered *and* Manhattan Unfurled. *Goldberger is currently working on a book about the experience of looking at architecture.*

19

nobu

1

Drawing upon chef Nobu Matsuhisa's origins in rural Japan, Rockwell Group worked with a palette of natural materials to create a space where the environment is elevated to the level of performance. In 2,800 square feet, neutral tones are accented by dashes of color, such as the *Madame Butterfly*–inspired cherry blossoms stenciled on the pale beechwood floors. The backlit bar is made of pea-green onyx and topped by scorched wood that is highlighted with bronze and polished brass. Accentuating the theatricality of Nobu, the sushi bar is set up much like a Kabuki theater stage. Behind a proscenium of floor-to-ceiling river rock, the chefs become actors and the patrons become the audience. The walls provide textured backdrops to this scene. One is covered with hundreds of shimmering

Japanese riverbed stones, while others reflect abstract sushi shapes, finished in paperlike ceramic tiles and rusted steel. Rockwell Group received an Annual Design Award for Nobu from *I.D.* magazine in 1995.

Four years after designing Nobu, Rockwell Group collaborated on Next Door Nobu, a smaller neighboring space of 1,300 square feet. Recalling the paragon of noodle shops from the movie *Tampopo,* Rockwell Group created an intimate and comfortable restaurant using many of the same design materials used in the original Nobu. A glowing bar is made of sake bottles, and a curving wall covered with *yakinori* (dried seaweed) represents the blending of food and space.

Following the success of the New York Nobus, a third restaurant opened

in the Hard Rock Hotel in Las Vegas in 1999. While sharing some design elements with its east coast counterparts, Nobu Las Vegas has a distinctive identity, in part because it is housed in a larger space of five thousand square feet. Helping to define dining areas within the restaurant are delicate bamboo screens, which sit within beds of river rock and disappear into the ceiling. Like the original Nobu, the face of the bar is backlit green onyx, but here green crackled tile adds a sparkling element and highlights the antique bronze top. The bar area sits within a pocket near the entry, where Japanese textiles hung in wall recesses float over glowing lights. *Hospitality Design* magazine chose Nobu Las Vegas for a Gold Key Award in 2000.

1 next door nobu
2 main dining room, nobu
3 sushi bar, nobu
4 birch column detail, nobu
5 birch column colonnade, nobu

Restaurants
New York City, Las Vegas
1994–1999

23

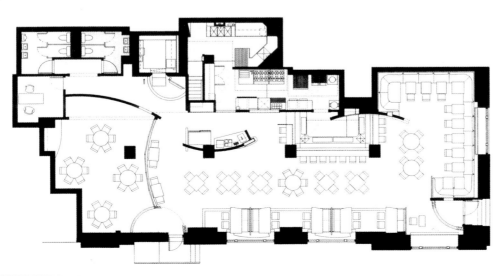

"When all is said it's got to look l

Drew Nieporent on Next Door Nobu, *New York Times,* February 19, 1998

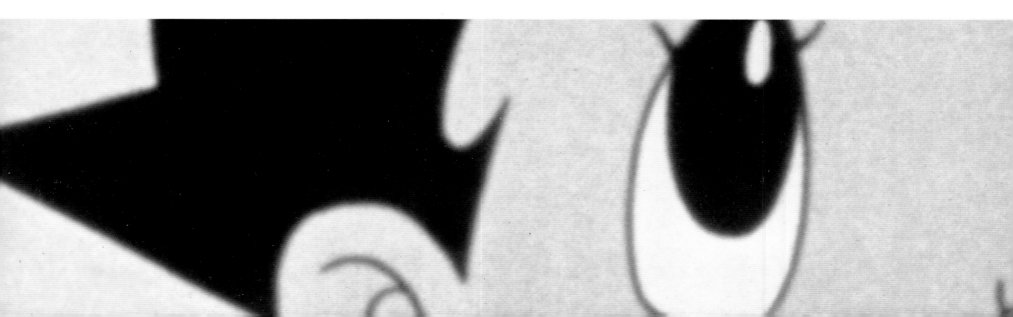

and done,
ke seaweed."

27

nobu

4

29

vong

1

ว่าง ทาง

ลงทุน (BOI) ปรับโครงการ

ประกอบการ ยุครัฐบาลชุดนี้

การปรับปรุงกฎเกณฑ์การ

หรือลดหย่อนภาษีการลงทุน

ประเทศนี้เป็นที่น่าดึงดูดของ

The design of Vong, named for chef Jean-Georges Vongerichten, synthesizes elements of Thai and continental culture while paying tribute to the chef's style of French-Thai cuisine. Upon entering, guests are met by a golden-hued collage, reminiscent of the work of Gustav Klimt but fashioned from fragments of daily life in Thailand: stamps, maps, newspapers, currency, matchbook covers, boxing programs, and train tickets, as well as bits of lemongrass and gold-leafed seashells. Thai architectural elements are adapted on a variety of scales in the dining room. A tatami platform provides an exclusive yet open dining area, while on another side of the dining room, an alcove known as the King's Booth is covered in traditional Thai plaid and enclosed by an oversized, curved screen

of iridescent gold, green, and blue mosaics. Tulip-shaped, hand-blown pendant lamps cast a soft pink light from above, calling to mind the Thai Festival of Lights and creating a dreamlike atmosphere in the 125-seat space.

The same theme received a more modern interpretation in Chicago's Vong restaurant. Rockwell Group created a 150-seat restaurant that gives a contemporary twist to the traditional forms and religious elements of Thailand, resulting in a space that is both serene and warm. From the street, one is drawn by the glow emanating from within; inside, light is gathered and shaped by glass-encased fabric panels, and a wall of mica torchères flickers invitingly. The platinum-wrapped dropped ceiling

hovers like a luminescent cloud over the dining space. Behind the maître d'hôtel stand, a vertical representation of an offering table with a polychromatic collage of some 150 spices alludes to the range of Vongerichten's cooking. Inspired by Thai architecture, a handcrafted board and baton wall of celadon-hued sycamore wood towers in the main dining room. More intimate private dining spaces, filled with natural silk pillows and set on bamboo tatami platforms, are visible through openings in the wall.

1 spice wall, chicago
2 king's booth, new york city
3 spice table and collage wall, new york city

Restaurant
New York City (Haverson / Rockwell Architecture), Chicago
1992, 1999

33

35

pod

pod

For this Asian-fusion restaurant on the campus of the University of Pennsylvania, Rockwell Group created a space inspired by a wide array of retro-futurist visual cues, ranging from Woody Allen's *Sleeper* to *The Jetsons* to the organic architectural and furniture forms of Eero Saarinen. The eight-thousand-square-foot room is marked by a series of womblike pod enclosures, from pods for two along the wall to pods for six to ten people that feature internally illuminated, color-changing ceilings. The bar area of Pod is highlighted by ottomans that glow when guests sit down and by a red platform made from polyurethane-coated foam, intended as an interactive sculptural piece for lounging. Incorporating the visual language of Stanley Kubrick's *2001,* cutting-edge materials are used throughout the restaurant. The bar is made from a translucent amber resin with a concrete bar dye; custom-made dining chairs are crafted from molded fiberglass; the partition separating the private dining area is silicone tubing; and the bathroom doors are frosted translucent urethane panels. For its design at Pod, Rockwell Group received a 2001 Lumen Award, as well as a nomination for Best Restaurant Design in 2001 by the James Beard Foundation.

1 bar, lounge
2 dining areas
3 sushi bar, dining pod
4 chroma control panel
5 window pod

Restaurant
Philadelphia
2000

39

pd

2 3

41

pod

43

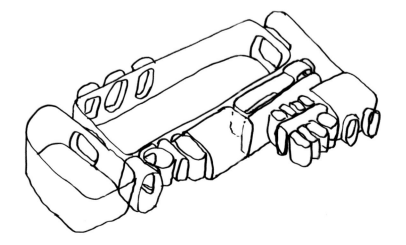

ruby foo's

1

With the design of Ruby Foo's, Rockwell Group playfully references the once-grand food emporiums of New York's Chinatown. But like the menu, the ten-thousand-square-foot space is in fact a tribute to the myriad Asian influences woven into the fabric of Western culture. The restaurant's two-story interior features a sweeping, curved black staircase that is set against the backdrop of a thirty-foot-high red-lacquered wall. Like an oversized Japanese bento box, the wall contains compartments that display objects (ranging from everyday bamboo steamers to an antique Buddha) gathered from countries across Asia. Throughout the restaurant, eclectic design elements symbolize the meeting of East and West. Hundreds of hanging mah-jongg

tiles form a glittering screen separating the bar area from the staircase, and tabletops employ the striking icono-graphy of Mott Street's neon signs. Colorful Chinese lanterns hang from above, while the white walls of the two-story sushi bar glow softly like the paper lanterns of Japan. In 2000, *Hospitality Design* magazine recognized Rockwell Group's design at Ruby Foo's with a Gold Key Award.

1 buddha, bento box wall
2 dining rooms with stair
3 bento box wall
4 backlit mah-jongg tile, bar

Restaurant
New York City, Upper West Side
1999

47

foo's

49

"Mr. Rockwell se
had Auntie Mam
he created that s
curved staircase

Ruth Reichl on Ruby Foo's, *New York Times,* March 24, 1999

just see her floa
crying 'Live, live,

ting down it,
live!'"

foo's

micha

el jordan's

michael jordan's

1 2

Overlooking Grand Central Terminal's main concourse, Michael Jordan's opened as part of a larger renovation with the restaurant occupying a portion of the north and west balconies. In order to achieve an intimate environment within the soaring seven-thousand-square-foot space, Rockwell Group erected a series of screen walls to divide the area into smaller sections, mediating between the scale of the terminal and the scale of a restaurant. Incorporating multiple details from the Raymond Loewy–designed Twentieth-Century Limited—the embodiment of the Golden Age of rail travel—the space has the streamlined elegance of art deco interiors. A curved mahogany wall is crowned with a dramatically lit metal leaf cornice, echoing the beaux arts majesty of the terminal, while the heavy velvets and hand-worn leathers of the furniture evoke the ambience of a dining club car. Illumination comes from the grand chandeliers that hang in the center of the terminal as well as lamps with orange-toned mica shades and a backlit mica bar. Surrounded by the cathedral-like opulence of the station, Michael Jordan's diners can gaze at the celestial ceiling above or watch the bustle of New York below. The restaurant received an Annual Interiors Award from *Interiors* magazine in 1999.

1 main dining room
2 private dining
3 balcony dining
4 private dining portal

Restaurant
New York City
1998

57

59

rosa

mexicano

rosa mexicano

For Josefina Howard's second New York restaurant, Rockwell Group blended contemporary Mexican architecture and art with traditional themes. Planar surfaces and vibrant colors inspired by the work of architect Luis Barragán are combined with textured and hand-crafted elements that evoke Mexican markets. Set in a dramatic two-story space, the Rockwell Group design features a thirty-foot water wall covered in mosaic tile of iridescent blue glass. Producing a sensation of being under-water, the tile colors range from lavender to cobalt to pale sky blue. In front of this waterfall, two hundred miniature sculptures of Acapulco cliff divers are arrayed perpendicular to the wall. The numerous figurines call to mind collections of folk art and votives traditionally found in Mexican homes. In addition to the installation of divers by artists Guido Grunenselder and Francesca Zwicker, artworks that evoke the land and bounty of Mexico are displayed, such as artist Michael Palladino's wax-covered wall map of Mexico, on which softly abstracted images of roses and corn are super-imposed. Artist Brad Oldham's wall-mounted art boxes of hammered metal tiles house images of pomegranates, beans, and other ingredients found in Mexican cuisine. Referencing the restaurant's name, roses were suspended in acrylic to create glowing walls in the bar area that connect the interior with the exterior. From the out-side, thirty-five-foot light towers based on the five spice gods make Rosa Mexicano the most visible building on the block. Rockwell Group received a 2001 Annual Interiors Award for Rosa Mexicano from *Interiors* magazine.

1 terrazzo stair with water wall
2 hand-tiled bar dye with backlit
  rose petal panels
3 wax-tiled mosaic, dining room
4 under floating terrazzo stair
5 second-floor dining

Restaurant
New York City
2000

63

rosa mexicano

65

2 | 3

67

animat

or's palate

In its signature restaurant for Disney Cruise Line, Rockwell Group wanted diners to experience the animator's process of creativity. At Animator's Palate, a four-thousand-square-foot restaurant, diners witness an animator's drawing in progress. Over the course of the meal, pen-and-ink sketches on the walls gradually shift to full-color drawings, creating the illusion of dining within an animated feature film. By the final course, the whole room dances with brilliant hues. Emphasizing the theme of concept-to-film, the structure's columns are reinterpreted as illuminated paintbrushes, and oversized painter's palettes are suspended overhead. On a smaller scale, each dining table has a centerpiece composed of paintbrushes in a vase. During dinner, the tips of the brushes begin to glow in multiple colors through fiber-optic technology. Even the waitstaff undergo a metamorphosis, beginning service in black-and-white attire, but changing into colorful costumes before bringing out dessert.

1 finish details
2 monochromatic concept drawing
3 color transformation

Restaurant
Disney Cruise Line, *Disney Magic* and *Disney Wonder*
1998 and 1999

71

A SMILE AND A SENSE OF DELIGHT
GAEL GREENE

I was an early obsessed foodie, a decade or so ahead of America's sensuality explosion when suddenly even the most puritan of affluent diners dared to discover that dinner could be more than well-done lamb chops and tapioca pudding. I'm an eater. I want my tuna tartare to sing a chorus in my mouth. I am beguiled by a hurricane of truffle thins flying into my creamy tagliolini, or by a perfect scallop in a pool of pungent sea urchin. But a great meal like great sex like great design plays to *all* our senses—looks good, feels good, smells good, sounds good . . . maybe even makes you giggle. In our sometimes cruel and uptight world, creative chefs and designing voluptuaries sense our craving for overwhelming pleasure.

Even in the pre-kiwi days before America's sensual revolution, Lutèce was supposed to evoke a sidewalk café off the Place du Furstenburg. Le Pavillion had red velour banquettes and murals by Jean Dufy, so all the haughty French Le's and La's draped themselves in red velour and sported evocative murals. Philip Johnson whipped out shimmering chain-mail curtains in the monumental Four Seasons. Joseph Baum's Forum of the Twelve Caesars had silver centurion helmets as ice buckets and Romulus and Remus espresso spoons that quickly vanished due to selective larceny. No one on the gourmand circuit in the seventies will quickly forget Sam Lopata's zebra chairs or the Japanese woodcut blowup of crashing waves over the sushi

bar at Seiyoken. By the time David Rockwell arrived from Guadalajara via Chicago, New Yorkers had come to expect—even appreciate—visual drama.

But Rockwell's school of fantasy kicked up the decibels. A piano player and tap dancer, he had drifted our way from an early passion for the theater. I have never watched him in the throes of creation but I can almost hear him saying, Let's imagine it's theater. Let's have fluorescent cobwebs and illuminated bats flying overhead (as they do at Le Bar Bat). Let's paint the back wall red and fill it with all the treasures of southeast Asia so the customers will be fighting to sit upstairs (as they do at Ruby Foo's uptown). Let's persuade them to be happy eating in the basement because it shimmers with strings of crystals that evoke water (as it does at Town).

Since dinner is theater for many Americans most days of the week, we expect to be transported and amused, to spend a few hours in another land or another decade. Ambitious restaurateurs are forced to think about design. And there are countless skilled hands in the trade. But Rockwell Group seems to have a special knack for creating an icon that expresses the personality, even the essence, of each place: Thailand's farms and city bustle are captured in the urbane Vong. A curved footbridge, fish swimming underfoot, and the rustic plaids of a Scandinavian fishing lodge all come together at Christer's. The cacophony of mah-jongg tiles, calligraphy on lacquered tables, giant color photographs of Chinatown Buddhas, Hong Kong neon, and a cheerful Mao signal Asian fusion at Ruby Foo's.

Nowhere are the images—the magic—more complex than at Nobu, with its astonishing wall of black river stones like a curving slab of Beluga, lit from below, that calls out to be touched. The sushi bar glows like the altar or stage set it is, with glowing onyx panels supporting the scorched wood counter and bar stools standing on chopstick feet. Why shouldn't a birch tree colonnade march through Nobu, leading toward the deep blue forest of stage scrim and birch branches? But having these real birch trunks carry light fixtures shaded with rusted steel plate and sprout solid ashwood branches strikes me as sheer Rockwell. Even the mattress-like sound mufflers take on a Zen position. It's impossible to walk into Nobu without a smile and a sense of delight.

Gael Greene has reviewed restaurants as New York *magazine's "Insatiable Critic" for more years than she will admit. She is the author of six books, two of them best-selling novels. With the late James Beard she cofounded and now chairs the board of Citymeals-on-Wheels, delivering meals to the homebound elderly.*

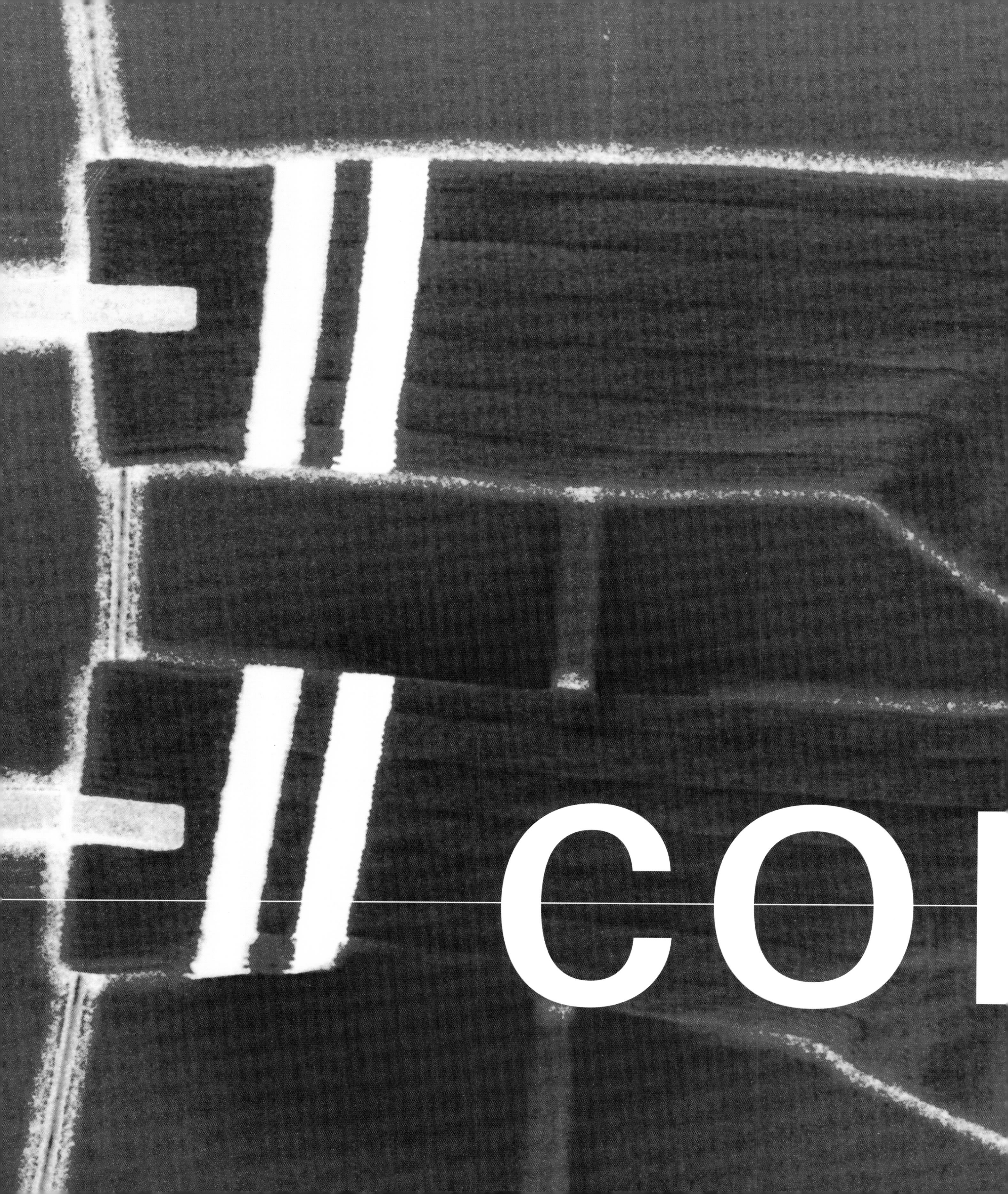
CO

nfort

Architectural practice is a complex and forcefully gregarious endeavor. It involves, to begin with, a cast of dozens of characters, from the architect and his collaborators to the client and his advisers and relatives, with an army of contractors in tow. A successful architect needs to have, beyond talent and patience, the synthesis and single-mindedness of a movie director or an army general. In this light, David Rockwell has a gift, a vision as complex as that of a Ridley Scott. Each Rockwell Group wonder is akin to a big Hollywood production. Not only are the credits endless, they are very public, and the roles that contributors play are always different from those played by their predecessors in other projects.

When it comes to the inspiration and the ingredients of each project, Rockwell's gift of synthesis is equally wondrous. What makes his architecture popular and entertaining is the choice of a theme and the myriad details that come together in the final choreography. The eyes never experience a dull moment, while the main theme of each new project shines through and guarantees a dramatic sense of ensemble. To take his milestone Nobu restaurant as an example, the visual references run wild among dueling samurai swords atop the sushi bar, long birch branches and scorched wood, one thousand Japanese riverbed stones on the wall, and the treelike floor-to-ceiling lighting sculptures—to name only a few features.

The 2,800-square-foot restaurant, completed in August 1994 for restaurant impresario Drew Nieporent, involved seventeen companies other than the client, the architects, the consultants, and the contractor. The contributors ranged from industrial manufacturers such as Thonet to craftsmen and artists. The orchestration of such a diverse group, in the fortunate absence of a repetitive style, represents Rockwell Group's unique signature. Even though Rosa Mexicano, Vong, Pod, and the W and Chambers hotels are very different from each other, they are all recognizable in their unique compositional approach. Energy and endless curiosity drive David Rockwell in his restless exploration of materials and ideas. His compositional and eclectic approach, moreover, makes him an emblem of contemporary creativity. Rockwell does not have a style, but rather communicates the joy and the pleasure that come from invention and from the alliance of many creative minds.

The emancipation from stylistic tyranny is one of the biggest achievements of the past decades. The acknowledgment that one style cannot fit all, a consequence of the revolutions of the twentieth century, has deep cultural implications and has contributed to reinforce both local and global culture alike. Style is today a matter of composition, in urban fashion as much as in urban architecture. Hip-hop music, with its emphasis on sampling and composing new and preexisting tracks and giving them a finishing varnish of surprising novelty, is the paradigm. Likewise, the Grands Travaux initiated by François Mitterrand in Paris in the 1980s, one of the most ambitious politico-architectural makeovers in our recent history, were a triumph of visual diversity, a sampling of new architectural landmarks.

Through what he calls his "narrative collages" of different materials and inspirations, which are physically gathered in tableaux at his office, Rockwell searches for that delightful moment, and for that delightful place, when different elements collide. Through the brainstorming phase with a multitude of collaborators, he approaches each project as an exercise in storytelling. Rockwell is keen on sampling and elaborating, curious about different cultures, and savvy in recognizing and applying talent. He invited actor Paul Reubens to brainstorm on a cruise ship for Disney, and Elizabeth Diller and Ricardo Scofidio on a project for Cirque du Soleil. He is known for calling in filmmakers, writers, and music composers to consult on different projects.

I asked David to describe one of his most recent works, the Chambers hotel in New York, in this light. In his office of about ninety people, there are three architectural studios assigned to different projects at any time. Storytelling requires discipline, and achieving Rockwell's ideal space, which he describes as "rooted in fantasy, rooted in reality," is not an easy walk. Rockwell confesses that he tries to keep himself off balance and his creativity alive by constantly changing project type. Likewise, he applies the same rule to his teams in order to motivate them. The teams vary in size—from two people for *The Rocky Horror Show* to thirty for the Mohegan Sun casino in Connecticut. The four people initially assigned to Chambers began brainstorming on the very narrow lot—50-by-120 feet—on West Fifty-sixth Street, to design Rockwell Group's first building from the ground up in New York. The owners, Ira Drukier, Richard Born, and Steven Caspi expressed a desire for a classic space. The Rockwell Group team set out to elaborate their proprietary version of eclectic classicism, as they defined it, by attempting to connect the building with its neighborhood and by devising new ways to interpret classic luxury.

According to Rockwell, there are always three points of attack that lead the project: the spatial program; the emotional design (content or theme); and the research into materials and elements. Chambers can be read according to these three plot lines. The narrow lot dictated the surprising multitiered space of the lobby and restaurant, where the architects forced the perspective farther using barrel vaults heading toward the skylight. The entrance elicits the emotion of a semiresidential downtown loft space, a typical New Yorker idea of luxury furnished with equally status-symbolic materials—concrete walls and leather-clad columns, fabrics inspired by Gucci, Prada, and Armani's latest collections—

handcrafted into position. The loft would not be complete without a dramatic two-story fireplace, which anchors the space, and an abundant amount of contemporary art. There are more than 250 artworks curated by Rockwell Group. Art becomes an even stronger protagonist on the upper floors, where each landing and corridor features a site-specific installation, and each of the seventy rooms has original art in it.

Rockwell Group often takes inspiration from theater in order to achieve the right amount of functional drama. Chambers demonstrates a reliance on Rockwell's four main theatrical references: a stunning entrance, one that lets visitors feel as if they are entering a new world with a new set of rules; a sense of procession that makes walking around the space a unique experience; transformation, which lets visitors feel as if change in space were happening in front of their eyes; and a particular, endless attention to lighting. Thus Rockwell achieves unique contemporary spaces that express history and contemporaneity and yet reflect the material culture that generated them. These spaces can also be compared to movies in that they spark a sense of belonging, while they manage to carry us to places we have never visited before.

Rosa Mexicano, the second installment of this successful Mexican restaurant located in New York City, on Columbus Avenue, is a good example of Rockwell adapting his approach to an ethnic theme, but one that nonetheless never feels foreign. In his youth Rockwell lived in Guadalajara. He credits his memories of the marketplace and its colors, of the unique light, of the flavors and scents as guidance throughout this project. The spatial program was dictated by the connection to the second floor, which the architects achieved by surprisingly sacrificing a big area on the ground to make room for the dramatic—"hypnotic," as Rockwell describes it—eighteen-foot staircase that is the restaurant's central design feature. Inspired by the work of Luis Barragán, Rockwell wanted all the surfaces in the restaurant to be sun drenched, except for the wall leading upstairs, which is finished with cobalt blue tiles. His team then set out to look for the right combination of folk art—Mexico—and minimal repetition—New York—that would crown the staircase's presence. The right choice of art eluded him until six weeks before the restaurant's

scheduled opening, when he walked into the Pescepalla Docks Gallery in Tribeca and found the paintings of Guido Grunenselder and Francesca Zwicker, big blue paintings of baby Jesuses. After thinking twice about a Catholic theme of crucifixes, Rockwell, Grunenselder, and Zwicker set their minds on an ingenious and less controversial choice: two hundred cast-resin white *clavadistas*—as the famous cliff divers of Acapulco are known—positioned on the wall's tiles.

Anything that is visually evocative of the project at hand goes in Rockwell's catalog of ideas and components, once again illustrating his innate ability to create a new synthesis of old and new, of industrial and handcrafted, of here, there, and everywhere. At the same time irreverent, experimental, and extremely receptive to the soul of things, Rockwell proves very hard to label. "I am not really interested in being considered a minimalist," he admits, and he has proven this throughout his career.

Paola Antonelli is a curator in The Museum of Modern Art's department of architecture and design. She has served as a contributing editor and writer to numerous international architecture and design periodicals and lectures regularly on architecture and design around the world. Antonelli is currently at work on a book about the design of food.

77

chambers

chambers

Fine art, fashion, and film all play a role in the design of Chambers, a seventy-seven-room hotel in midtown Manhattan where luxurious materials provide a counterpoint to simple forms. The building was conceived as a fusion of townhouse and gallery. Its extroverted two-story lobby, entered through a pair of colossal "woven" wood doors, consists of a smaller scale "living room" nested within a soaring gallery-like volume. The dialogue of these competing sensibilities is played out through contrasts between rich and raw materials. Concrete columns are clad in leather, finished stone slabs are supported artfully on the stringer of the raw steel stair, and a table fashioned of rough anthracite coal rests on a rich Tibetan carpet. Original artwork adorns the lobby and permeates the hotel.

The corridor of each guest-room floor features an original installation by an emerging artist. Guest rooms, including one duplex and four suites, have the casual but dynamic feeling of artists' lofts. Leather-sheathed sawhorses support sheet-glass desks, and currents of color (grape- and kiwi-colored otto-mans, larkspur and orchid bedding) run throughout. In the bathrooms, inlaid handmade glass tiles and Italian bowl-mounted sinks play off rough concrete floors. On the lower level of the hotel, the restaurant Town is situated in an introverted two-story skylit atrium. The design of Town was inspired by Manhattan's pocket parks, idyllic spaces nestled between skyscrapers. Walls of backlit blond wood are set below panels covered in taupe suede. Curtains of glass beads

reflect light from the corners, giving the space a light, airy ambience. Rockwell Group received a 2001 Gold Key Award for Chambers from *Hospitality Design* magazine. The hotel was also honored by I.D. Magazine Annual Design Review in 2002.

1 lobby reception through bar
2 axonometric of chambers and town
3 stairway, town
4 lobby seating from mezzanine
5 town
6 detail of guest corridor
7 mezzanine lounge with
   library shelving
8 duplex
9 woven walnut entry doors

Hotel, Restaurant
New York City
2001

81

chambers

2

"14 Things to say and do

Bob+Roberta Smith 20

LETS

TH

BAS

THE

45

85

chambers

7

87

new york

w new york

1

Located in a building designed by Emery Roth in 1928, the W New York was conceived as an "Urban Oasis" in hectic midtown Manhattan. The entrance to the 720-room hotel makes a distinctive first impression with the clean lines of its stainless steel and glass canopy. As *Interior Design* magazine noted, "After dark, when fiber-optic spotlights raise specks of sparkle, the entire configuration brings to mind a species of sleek industrial sculpture." Protruding through the old building's skin, the canopy is a preview of the world that awaits the visitor inside. The interior lobby was conceived as an abstracted landscape—forest, canyon, and garden are expressed in a palette of natural materials; open spaces and mosaic-tiled windows emphasize airiness and light. The guest rooms expand upon this theme. The woven metal and wood headboard creates a vestibule to the room. The bed, in the center of the room, is dressed with custom linens embroidered with sayings that invite the guests to "Walk with Confidence" and "Sleep with Angels." Stenciled leaves and grass-filled window boxes are accompanied by watering cans. The concept of rejuvenation is further expressed in the hotel's health club, spa, and juice bar. The Heartbeat Restaurant and the Whiskey Blue Bar on the ground level add to the W New York guest experience. Rockwell Group received a 1999 Annual Design Award from *I.D.* magazine and a 2000 Annual Interiors Award from *Interiors* magazine for W New York.

1 lobby reception with dried
  flower wall
2 entry canopy
3 sleep quote bedding
4 mirrored mosaic columns,
  heartbeat restaurant
5 signature guest room
6 entry vestibule with
  headboard divider
7 column signage

Hotel
New York City
1998

91

w new york

541

W NEW YORK

2

...TD WITH ANGELS...

93

W

NEW YORK

6 7

BLUE

w ur

Rockwell Group's second W hotel design in New York City involved the revitalization of the Guardian Life Building, a twenty-story granite and limestone landmark dating from 1911. The building's architecture is emblematic of an age when Union Square was the center of New York fashion and society. Rockwell Group's design literally brings Union Square's park into the lobby and draws inspiration from the fashions of 1911, when a slit at the ankle of a woman's dress was considered revealing and sexy. The lobby was conceived as a light-filled conservatory. Colossal, sensuously curving topiary columns, and fitted Macore wood panels define a grand "urban living room" overlooking lower Park Avenue and Union Square. Inside, the focal point of the check-in area is a sweeping grand staircase of mahogany and limestone that rises dramatically to the historic second-floor ballroom. Wheatgrass grows in planters at the edge of each step and on top of the mahogany check-in desk adorned with mother-of-pearl inlay tiles. Architectural elements such as coffered ceilings, marble mosaic floors, and vaulted marble hallways were restored, while contemporary touches, such as beds covered in shiny sharkskin and topped by leather headboards, were added in the 220 guest rooms. Downstairs, Todd English's Olives restaurant and Rande Gerber's Underbar lounge draw visitors from outside the hotel. W Union Square won a *Business Week*–sponsored award in 2002.

1 guest check-in
2 grand staircase with wheatgrass detail
3 lobby living room
4 grand staircase
5 guest room with corset lighting
6 topiary wall, lobby

Hotel
New York City
2000

99

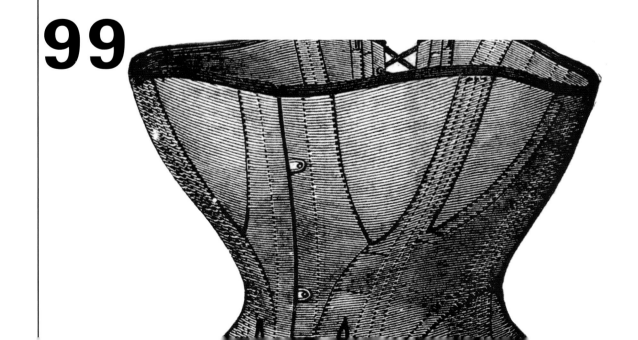

"We called in the

Edmond Bakos, Rockwell Group, on W Union Square, *USA Today*, February 9, 2001

horticulturalists..."

101

GUARDIAN

2 3

103

w union

quare

4

montefiore

montefiore

1

Guided by the concept that children are explorers on a journey to healing, the Children's Hospital at Montefiore provides the finest medical care to the children of the Bronx and southern Westchester County. Throughout the 106-bed hospital, the child is the focus and driving force behind Rockwell Group's design, which reflects both the philosophies of family-centered care and the teachings of Carl Sagan. Integrating a child's family into the care process was an important consideration when designing the hospital. Having family members close by creates an atmosphere of reassurance, nurturing, and support. In addition to their familial world, children's connection to the larger whole of the cosmos is stressed, making a hospital stay a journey not only toward healing, but also toward knowledge. Visitors find themselves immersed in an environment that reinforces their place in the universe, both in scale and location. For example, the "You Are Here" map shows humanity's location on a jumbo glass mural of the Milky Way galaxy. Rockwell Group chose both locally and nationally known artists to develop installations for each floor. The art is based on a specific idea that relates to either the developmental level of the child or illness treated on that floor. Because a hospital visit can be frightening for a child, curiosity and a sense of wonder are encouraged; a child's learning more about his or her condition may not only be fascinating but also empowering. A custom Intranet and supporting software help synthesize these ideas with the principles of the hospital, connecting a child in bed to a whole world of information and entertainment.

1 entry with lobby galaxy wall
  and ecosphere
2 terrazzo bridge leading
  to ecosphere
3 patient room
4 galaxy mosaic, sixth-floor
  elevator lobby
5 moon desk, suzanne pincus
  family learning center

Hospital
Bronx
2001

108

montefiore

STAR STUFF

2

1027

C100

6R

3 4

EXPLORER'S KIT

① JOURNAL
AGE APPROPRIATE

② EARTH
HAND EXERCISE
ALL AGES

③ PRISM
CHILDREN &
ADOLESCENTS

④ PERSONALIZED
MAGNETIC KEY
WRIST BAND
ALL AGES

⑤ COMPASS/
BINOCULARS
6 YRS +

⑥ PERISCOPE
4 YRS +

⑦ PLANT GROW KIT
6 YRS +

⑧ BUG VISION
MONOCLE
6 YRS +

⑨ DISCOVERY
CENTER DUFFEL
STAR
ALL AGES

⑩ FINGER PUPPETS
CHILDREN

⑪ CALLING CARD
ADOLESCENTS

⑫ FELT TOYS
YOUNG CHILDREN

⑬ PERSONALIZED
TRADING CARDS

Somehow, the dawn of the twenty-first century—no small feat for the planet—seems overshadowed by events born of a phenomenal disregard for humanity and basic decency. Who knows what will come of all of this? We are struggling with uncertainty and looking into a future that does not easily evoke orderly images of a world basking in peace and progress.

Whatever happens, several things are very clear. First of all, the cliché is true: the world is changing. Second, the changes for America are particularly profound. It's as if we were in a reverie of adolescence, suddenly shaken by extraordinary events, now forced to face reality, join the world, get connected to the rest of the planet . . . in a sense, forced to grow up overnight.

The third change may be a subtle—but critical—evolution in what we see when we look at our children. Perhaps what is truly precious is what children themselves possess, not what we see in them. They, after all, will cherish life or not; they will be inquisitive and open or intolerant and full of wrath. They will want to learn and explore or acquire and languish.

What turns the tide, this way or that, for children? It is of course more than we can fully grasp. It starts with DNA and parents and keeps going through teachers and mentors and the subtle infusion of humanity and spirituality. But it is always also about experiences, planned and unexpected. The Children's Hospital at Montefiore is, in this way, the creative product of people who were thinking hard about the concept of experience. We knew we would have a children's hospital that could be depended on—absolutely—to provide state-of-the-art medical care. That would go without saying. The question was, "Where could we go from there?"

There were two answers. One had to do with the notion that every modern pediatric hospital must be a physical and functional space that recognizes and celebrates the family—and the community. This meant making rooms comfortable for parents to stay with their children; creating an ambience that is familiar and comfortable, evocative of the values and images that encourage tranquility and security; and engaging parents in the processes of understanding and participating in solving the health challenges of their children.

Finally, there was an opportunity to do something that would potentially recast the idea of what could be achieved in a specialized facility for children. We wanted to fundamentally change the expectations and redefine the experience of what happens during treatment and recovery. These are capturable moments. But for what purpose?

I had been a close friend of the preeminent scientist and teacher Carl Sagan for fifteen years before his untimely death in 1996. His life had been devoted to seeking truth and sharing the joy of exploration and discovery with millions of people in every corner of the globe. And he especially loved the idea of how easy it is to inspire children with moments of wonder and insight. To me, this was the big idea. The Bronx is still one of the most medically underserved urban communities in the nation. That is precisely where we would build a children's hospital that would provide both excellence in health care and a total environment that would ignite the imagination of children.

Who could do this? Surely not the typical hospital designer. We turned to Rockwell Group and asked if they could help us create an integrated set of spaces that would infuse a sense of beauty and inspiration into the entire hospital, from the lobby to the pediatric intensive care unit on the top floor. With extraordinary exhibits, the interpretive work of many artists, and a team working on a unique bedside-operated interactive system for children and families, Rockwell Group's design concept worked.

Any hospital is, at its core, about healing. This one, for children, is also about discovery and exploration of the world and of oneself. Surely, in the years to come, we'll successfully treat many, many children. With any luck, we'll also change some lives in ways that may cast a spell of hope and possibility. Just what the doctor ordered.

Dr. Irwin Redlener is president and cofounder of The Children's Health Fund. At Montefiore Medical Center he is president of the Children's Hospital and director of community pediatrics. He is also professor of pediatrics at the Albert Einstein College of Medicine and lecturer in pediatrics at Harvard Medical School.

Whether you're an exhausted road warrior stranded on a layover in Dayton, Ohio, or a nervous hospital patient facing something considerably more frightening, you will likely agree that most hotel and hospital environments share one common trait: they have been designed, however unintentionally, to exacerbate the situation. Anyone who's spent time in both can tell you that hospitals and hotels have a lot in common. Both are "homes away from home" that are in reality anything but. Both are furnished in much the same manner. There is a relentless sameness that unites both environments.

Consider the uncomfortable bed facing the immovable television, or the inappropriate chairs and inadequate side tables that never seem to be in the right position no matter how often you reposition them. And the hopelessly inept attempts to add "warmth"—the blurry seascapes, the cheaply framed exhibition posters—that always seem half-hearted and after-the-fact. Some might say the lockstep predictability of these places is calculated to reassure. Others might point out that standardization also conveniently suits an accountant's view of the bottom line. In any case, if surprise, drama, and delight nourish the human experience, hotels and hospitals put their visitors on a starvation diet.

Into this lifeless milieu comes the Chambers hotel in Manhattan and the Children's Hospital at Montefiore in the Bronx. At Chambers, there are surprises everywhere, from the massive but gently yielding lobby doors to the desks in the rooms (each is made of a sheet of heavy glass that rests on a wooden sawhorse) to what is surely the most unforgettable touch, the hallway art installations, different for each floor and executed by emerging artists. Even after a few bottles of wine downstairs at the Rockwell Group–designed Town restaurant, a guest of Chambers will never forget whether they're spending the night on the eighth floor, with its exuberant garden mural painted by John Newsom, or the ninth, with its thousands of tiny mirrors dangling from the walls—an installation by artist Alyson Shotz.

Similarly, Rockwell Group's work for Montefiore makes a memorable event out of an experience that many of its guests would probably like to forget. Unlike the typical hospital environment, the passive nature of which often gives one a feeling of helplessness, Montefiore is full of surprises that seek to transform the experience into an active one. For their first hospital project—a children's hospital—Rockwell Group conceived not just architectural experiences (interactive maps, a domed planetarium) but personal ones as well (they proposed kits and passports that each child is given to guide them through their "journey to healing"). And as at the Chambers hotel, art meets real life at Montefiore. Rockwell Group brought in the artist Tom Otterness, who designed the hospital's Foucault pendulum, and Tracy Dockray, who is responsible for the facility's user-friendly signage system with its playful font.

In the end, when you check out of the Chambers hotel or Montefiore, you enter the streetscape relieved knowing that—finally—someone has figured out what to do with these environments, that there can be a positive relationship between a hotel and a hospital. In the case of these two spaces designed by Rockwell Group, the glue of their relationship consists of tastefully executed visual stimulation combined with an unusually high level of comfort.

Michael Bierut is a partner in the New York office of the international design consultancy Pentagram. He is a past president of the American Institute of Graphic Arts and a senior critic at the Yale University School of Art.

113

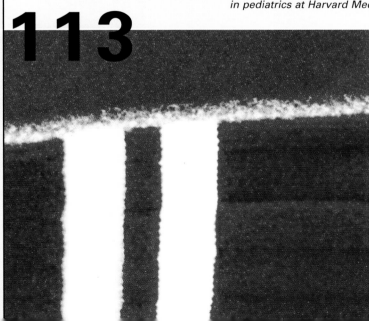

stim

est cellars

APPLE CRISP
BOCCADIGABBIA GARBI 1995

Do you love the tart mouthwatering crunch of a perfectly ripe Granny Smith? Does the notion of fruity, yet refreshingly tangy wine that tastes like green apples and bosc pears sound appealing? We thought so.

WHAT? CHARDONNAY AND TREBBIANO
WHERE? MARCHES, ITALY
FYI: A GREAT CRISP CLEAN WHITE FROM ITALY

206

$9.99

ORANGE BLOSSOM SPECIAL
RIZZARDI SOAVE CLASSICO 1995

Forget everything you ever thought about Soave being a little jug wine. Tuck your nose into a glass of this petal-scented beauty and you'll sing its praises—with or without a banjo and country fiddle.

WHAT? TREBBIANO & GARGANEGA
WHERE? VENETO, ITALY
FYI: THE VENETO IS ALSO THE HOME OF PROSECCO

$7.49

FROM UMBRIA, WITH LOVE
POGGIO DEL LUPO ORVIETO 1995

This graceful, light-as-a-feather, mouthwatering fresh white wine betrays the notion that Orvieto need always taste like thin, sharp, backward-leaning plonk. Poggio del Lupo's is anything but!

WHAT? TREBBIANO
WHERE? UMBRIA, ITALY
FYI: A GREAT WINE FOR VIN-DRESSED SALADS

$9.99

HUNGARIAN RHAPSODY
CHATEAU PAJZOS TOKAJI 1993

e most famous wines from Hungary's all region are quite sweet, but this one all about being crisp and dry. It's said wines of Tokaji were the last Czar's ite drink. At least he had good taste!

WHAT? FURMINT
WHERE? TOKAJI, HUNGARY
TOKAJI, THE REGION, HAS NO RELATION TO TOKAY, THE GRAPE

$8.99

MILK AND HO
HAGAFEN HARMON

best cell

fizzy   fresh   soft

luscious   Ⓑ   juicy

smooth   big   sweet

Intended as the prototype for a national chain, the design of Best Cellars seeks to take the mystery—but not the allure—out of buying wine. Rather than offer a bewildering array of vintages, Best Cellars focuses on a carefully curated selection whose presentation seeks to simplify the buying process. In approximately one thousand square feet, a combination of American Sycamore wood accents, hand-rubbed burgundy plaster walls, and gray, polished concrete flooring provide a perfect backdrop for the bottles' dazzling constellation of colors. Wines are grouped not by region or grape type but instead by taste and style, under categories such as "smooth," "big," and "luscious," and each wine is accompanied by a succinct, often humorous description of its flavor and origin. The overall result is an innovative brand image unique to Best Cellars. By creating both a playful and practical approach to buying wine, Rockwell Group demystifies the process for the consumer and, as a result, sets Best Cellars apart from others in its category. This successful formula was repeated in additional Best Cellars stores on the East Coast and in Seattle. Rockwell Group received a 1998 Lumen Award for Best Cellars from the Illuminating Engineering Society and a citation for interior architecture from the American Institute of Architects.

1 wine display and shelf-talker
2 interior

Retail Wine Shop
New York City; Boston and Brookline, Massachusetts; Seattle; Washington, D.C.
1996–2001

121

FIZZY

SPARKLING WINES

FRESH

LIGHT-BODIED WHITE WINES

SOFT

LUSCIOUS

BEST CE

best cellars

INWORP
3 GULDENS
FL. 3.00

FEBO

morgentha

l-frederics

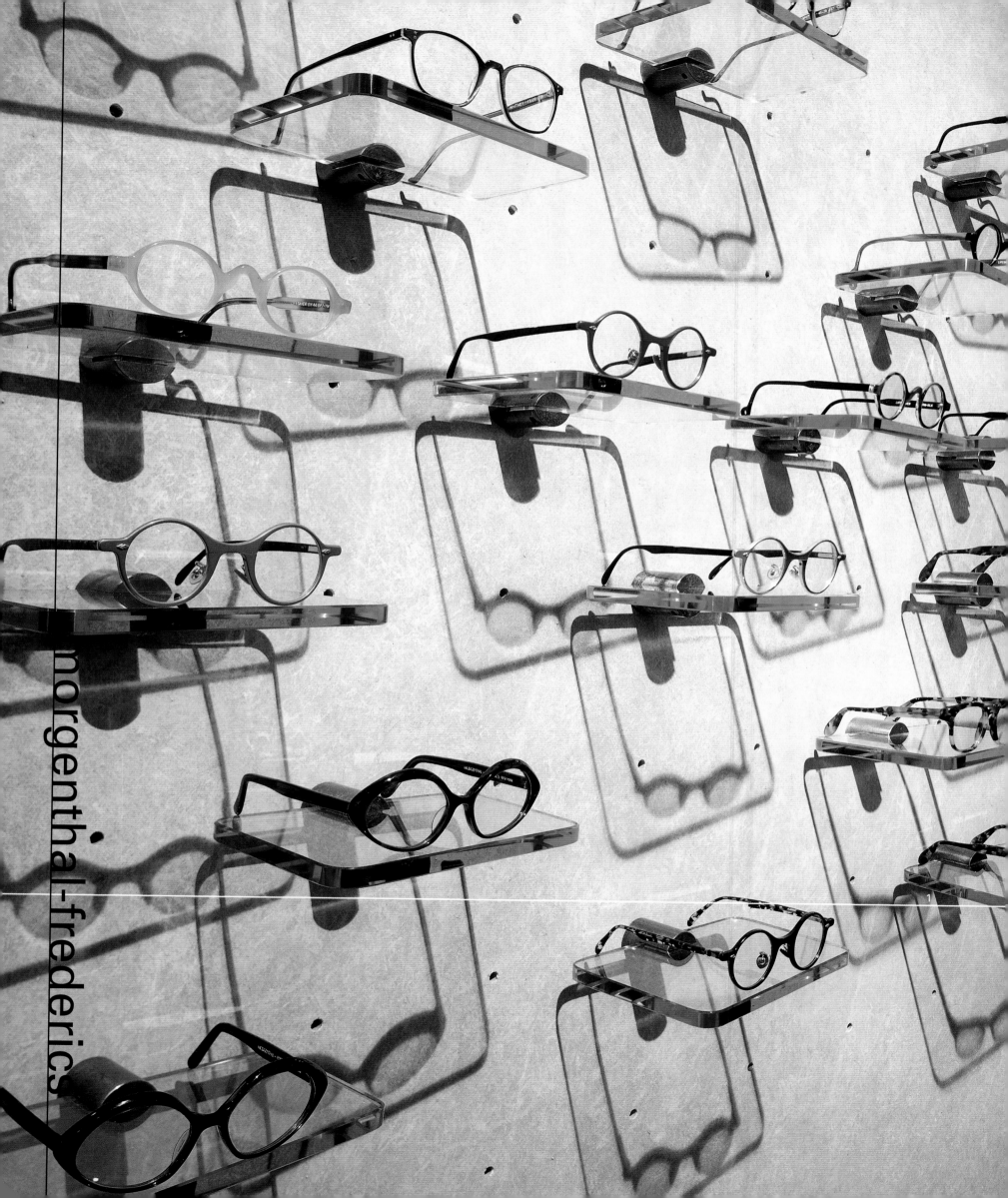

morgenthal-frederics

The design for the three New York stores of Morgenthal-Frederics embodies the craftsmanship and detail found in the store's own eyewear. To create a functional yet sensual environment, Rockwell Group drew inspiration from Shaker and other American craft influences, the display cases of old pharmacies, and the art boxes of Joseph Cornell. In the small spaces of five to six hundred square feet, part of the challenge was fashioning proper displays for the eyewear. The solution was custom cases, constructed from elements found in the eyeglasses themselves, which position the frames in unexpected ways. Oversized pieces of furniture together with overscaled mirrors allude to eyeglass shapes and create a "through the looking glass" illusion. Custom lighting evokes the tortoiseshell pattern of classic eyeglass frames. By mixing nostalgic references and innovative display techniques, the design allows patrons to see eyewear in a new way.

1 eyeglass display wall
2 shaker-inspired cabinetry
3 collage box window display, madison avenue
4 store interior, madison avenue

Opticians (three locations)
New York City
1994–1998

127

morgenthal-frederics

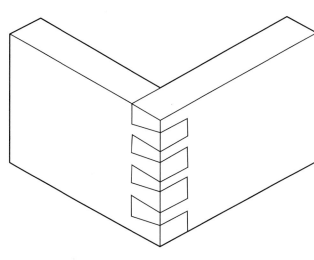

129

jerse

y gardens

gardens

For Jersey Gardens, a two-story, 1.5-million-square-foot retail, shopping, and entertainment complex in Elizabeth, New Jersey, Rockwell Group created the unexpected: a garden oasis. The design transformed a bleak industrial setting along the New Jersey Turnpike into a lush natural environment. Marsh grasses (native to the area) are planted at the edge of the site, and the abstract notion of "garden" continues within. Skylights allow natural light into the center court, which is conceived as a "vertical garden," surrounded by two three-hundred-foot long and forty-foot tall topiary walls. In the middle, a "tree-house," with bridges connecting the upper levels, sits beside an abstract waterfall made of slanted translucent panels. Secondary courts follow the same theme, such as the "Celestial Garden," which features internally illuminated birch trees. The carpeting in this area, with alternating bands of light and dark green, mimics twice-mown grass. The main mall pathways are marked by topiary arches and have suspended light fixtures reminiscent of the strings of lights used for a village festival (inspired by Little Italy's annual San Gennaro Festival). With seating areas composed around a series of wood and steel lattice structures, the food court recalls an informal plaza on the edge of a hill town.

1 treehouse in center court
2 rusted steel and chain link
  topiary wall
3 resin tree forest, end court

Retail Center
Elizabeth, New Jersey
1999

133

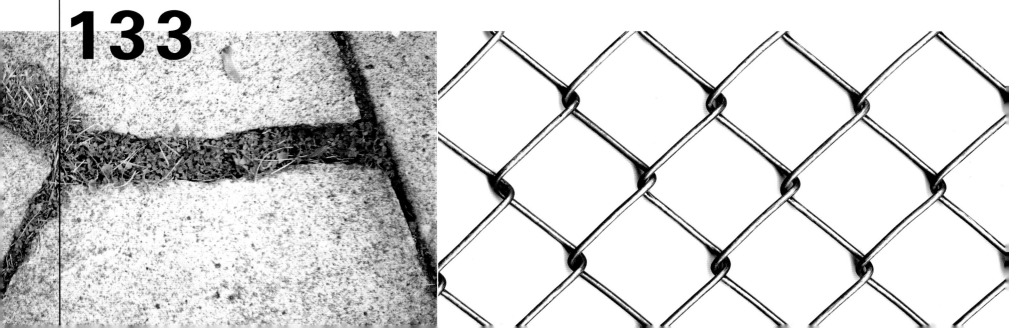

2

events

the great bazaar

Inspired by the labyrinthine markets found in such countries as Morroco and Mexico, The Great Bazaar was an experiment in combining retail and theater for Design Industries Foundation Fighting Aids (DIFFA). Set inside a temporary tent erected at Lincoln Center's Damrosch Park, the Middle Eastern–style Bazaar was a tapestry of lush colors and exotic patterns, with stylized minarets and glittering beads. The shopping areas of the twenty-thousand-square-foot Bazaar offered an array of goods for purchase. In addition, a silent auction was held, featuring handmade items such as pillows designed by artists and celebrities, including Todd Oldham, Cindy Crawford, Robert De Niro, Dustin Hoffman, Julie Taymor, and Dale Chihuly. Food catered by Rosa Mexicano and Payard Patisserie and Bistro among others added to the sumptuous ambience, while perform-ances by Cyndi Lauper and Cirque du Soleil lent an atmosphere of a carnival. Graphic artist Stefan Sagmeister designed invitations and signage for the event, complete with arabesques and charmed snakes. David Rockwell was elected Chairman of the Board of Trustees of DIFFA in 2000.

1 beaded entry curtain
2 bazaar market shops
3 double snake stage with cyclorama

Event
Benefit for Design Industries Foundation Fighting AIDS (DIFFA)
Damrosch Park, Lincoln Center
New York City
2000

green

bazaar

2 · 3

Conceived as part of a benefit for Design Industries Foundation Fighting Aids (DIFFA), Rockwell Group's fantasy library for the actor Jeremy Irons is a romantic view of the Victorian period with a revisionist twist. Irons had offered a quote from Yeats as the inspiration for his dream space: "We can make our minds so like still water that beings gather about us that they may see, it may be, their own images. And so live for a moment with a clearer, perhaps with a fiercer life because of our quiet." Rockwell Group envisioned the room as a bucolic space encountered during a walk in the woods. The library is covered by a gazebo-like structure supported by eight groups of columns. Upon closer inspection, the columns are made from tree trunks with soaring bronze branches. Through details like these, the intimate interior space has the feeling of the outdoors in autumn. Contributing to this feeling are a patch of grass, a wine-colored velvet floor quilt dappled with appliquéd leaves, and golden flocked wallpaper with an inverted tree pattern that conveys a sensation of floating.

1 library lounge
2 view of installation
3 rose window

Metropolitan Home Street of Shops to benefit
Design Industries Foundation Fighting AIDS (DIFFA)
New York Design Center
New York City
1994

jeremy irons library

US THAT THEY MAY SEE , IT MA...

...AN... ...OR A MOMENT WITH

irons library

WE CAN MAKE OUR MINDS SO LIKE STILL
WATER THAT BEINGS GATHER ABOUT US THAT THEY
MAY SEE, IT MAY BE, THEIR OWN IMAGES.

AND SO LIVE FOR A MOMENT WITH A CLEARER,
PERHAPS WITH A FIERCER LIFE BECAUSE OF
OUR QUIET.

Designed for the occasion of DIFFA's "Collection Rouge II: Dining by Design" in 1997, The Secret Garden display was inspired by Francis Hodgson Burnett's popular children's story of the same name. Surrounded by a halo of birch treetops, the circular structure suggests a private garden oasis for tranquil contemplation. Approaching the enclosure, the visitors were met with a garden wall of woven birch branches and grass. Once inside, they had stepped into a secluded glen with a circle of aged wooden benches and simple burlap and linen cushions clustered around a table. Fragrant sprigs of sage and rosemary emerged through the stones of the terraced tabletop, while votive candles glowed in the trees. With chargers made of fresh grass, twig-shaped flatware, and a champagne vessel constructed from a bird's nest, dinner guests felt as if they were in a garden that was just coming to life.

For DIFFA's 1998 Dining by Design event, Rockwell Group conceived the I Get a Kick from Champagne installation for Champagne Mumm as a miniature version of a luxe Busby Berkeley set. Mixing theater and reality in a glamorous setting, the design paid tribute to the most celebratory of drinks. An oversized ruby-red champagne bucket encircled by giant champagne flutes stood at the center of the table. Chargers of lush jewel-toned Mongolian lambs' wool rested on the silver and pale mint green of the glass mosaic tabletop. Draped in red and purple velvet, the table shone with beaded and mother-of-pearl utensils. A hundred hand-blown glass bubbles hung from above, capturing the effervescence of champagne.

1 The Secret Garden
2 I Get A Kick from Champagne

Installations
Dining by Design Benefit for Design Industries Fighting AIDS (DIFFA)
Metropolitan Pavilion
New York City
1997, 1998

diffa tables

i.d. exhibit

I.D. EXHIBITION

EXIT

1 2

concluding illustration represents a very large, | PLANETARIUM, invented and made by THOMAS H. BARLOW
ated, and ...ous piece of mechanism,—the | of Lexington, Kentucky. We cannot regard this a...

ASTRONOMY, INSTRUM,...

exhibit

...s ranking higher than a philosophical toy, and | authority of Sir John Herschel, in his Outlines of Ast...

Begun in 1954, the International Design Magazine Annual Design Review is America's oldest and most prestigious juried design recognition competition. Over two thousand products and projects in eight categories—consumer products, furniture, graphics, equipment, concepts, environments, packaging, and student work—represent the best designs produced in the past year. Invited by the magazine's editor to design an exhibition in 1997, Rockwell Group used the theme of orbiting planets to create an installation that highlighted each product's unique contribution while also emphasizing how the products related to one another. Blue walls surrounded the space, and the products were hung by aircraft cable varying in height from two-and-a-half to seven-and-a-half feet.

The products were arrayed as if they were part of a solar system, with the emanating fields of planetary "belts" representing product categories. Spotlights focused light on the winning products, like planets catching the brilliance of the sun.

1 stellar products
2 tensile product display

Exhibition Design
American Institute of Graphic Arts
New York City
1997

151

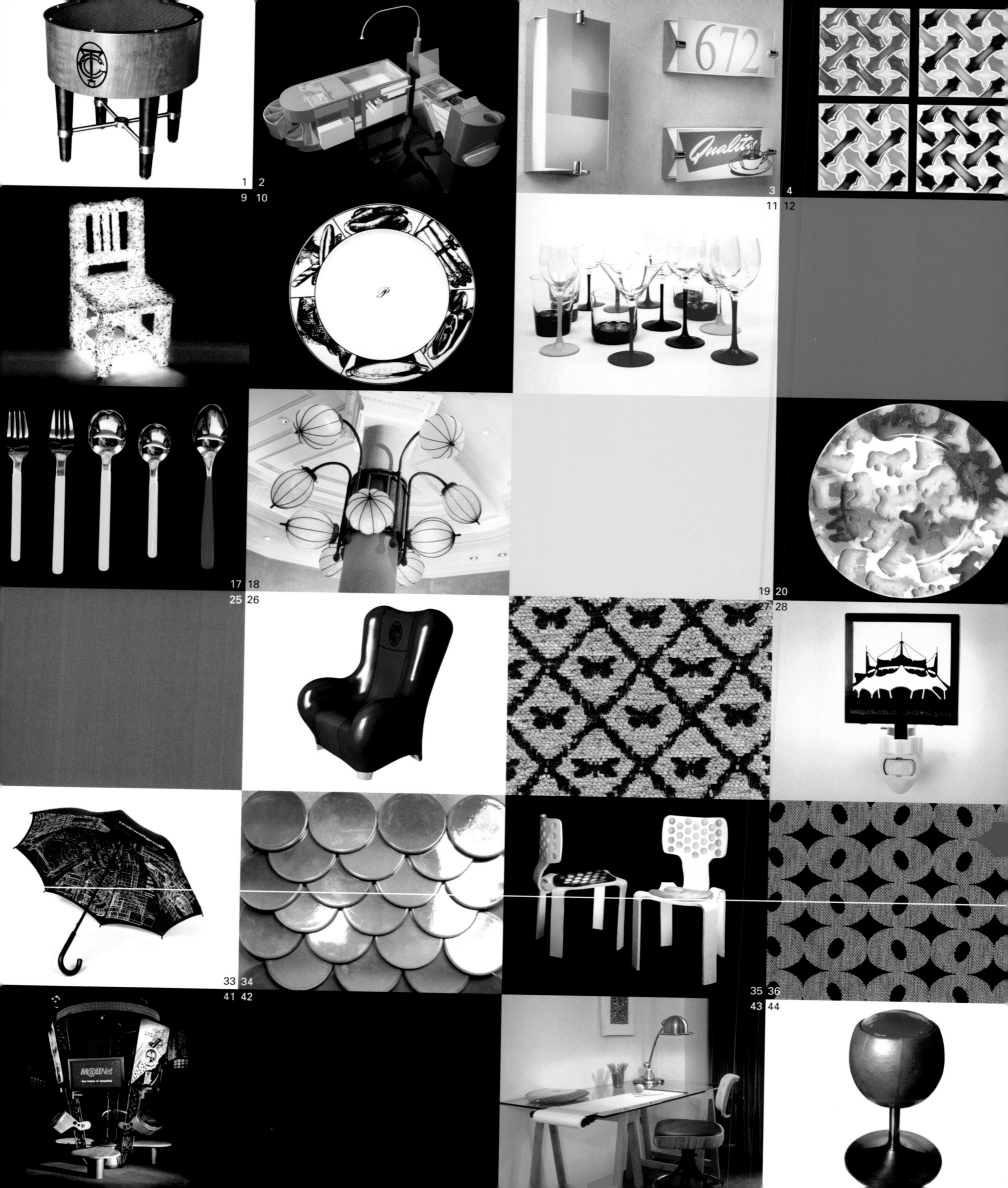

products

Rockwell Group designs total environments, from the architecture to the furniture, lighting and textiles. Designing for its own projects as well as for licensing, Rockwell Group combines innovative materials with familiar forms, creating products that can also stand alone as original design concepts. For example, in the high-traffic terminal of Grand Central Station, Rockwell Group wanted to create the feeling of an urban living room. Designers developed seating in the shape of overstuffed armchairs and loveseats; however, traditional form belies the fabric: durable custom-colored Corian. Other products listed below embody the same mix of convention and invention.

1 vitrine table, grand central terminal
2 thekitchensink, rockwell group
3 little ricky lighting, baldinger
4 glazed tiles, sultan's palace at desert passage
5 black
6 lounge bar, pod
7 skyline screen, monkey bar
8 love plates, fellissimo
9 illuminated beaded chair, world studio foundation
10 bistro plate, payard patisserie & bistro
11 rubber-dipped glassware, rockwell group
12 cyan
13 marble and metal light fixture, tribeca grill
14 magenta
15 pajama pattern, diffa
16 marcia chair, pace

17 rubber-dipped flatware, pod
18 whisk chandelier, payard patisserie & bistro
19 yellow
20 animal cracker plate, unesco
21 cast fiberglass chair, pod
22 fan lamp, vong
23 illuminated frame, newh
24 flocked wallpaper, strip house
25 magenta
26 molded corian chair, grand central terminal
27 moth textile, bronx zoo
28 night light, rockwell group
29 el table model, rockwell group
30 illuminated clock, world studio foundation
31 sleep quote bedding, w new york
32 woven crushed glass chandelier, steuben
33 blueprint umbrella, rockwell group

34 fish scale tiles, kingfish
35 gel chair concept, rockwell group
36 flip-flop textile, design tex
37 yellow
38 bistro flatware, payard patisserie & bistro
39 punched metal chandelier, tapika
40 lucite ottoman, chambers
41 interactive media station, m@llnet
42 black
43 trestle table, rockwell group
44 martooni olive stool, monkey bar
45 sushi chair, nobu
46 curiosity jar plate, unesco
47 cyan
48 plasma-charged martini glass, bombay sapphire

Custom and licensed product design
1990–2002

products

Conversation, conversation, conversation, conversation.

I love conversation.

I love conversation with others, with myself, with spaces and places.

Our most mystical moments are inner conversations with God in a place of worship. Prayers are conversations in an appropriate place. Such a place is designed to evoke a more honest, clearer, and thoughtful conversation. What do we say to ourselves in the Pantheon, Karnak, or Angkor Thom— and to the structure itself?

It is certainly evident that whales, porpoises, primates, and birds talk to each other (bees buzz and crickets click). We do not understand their systems of communication or memory. Nor do we understand how or even if their forms of literacy build connections between moments from year to year and generation to generation (beehives and anthills barely count). It is clear, however, that they do not create the spaces in which to have their conversations.

Lou Kahn, at the height of his creativity, wrote about having conversations with inanimate objects. "I asked a brick what it wanted to be. It said, 'I want to be an arch.'" He had these imaginary conversations with buildings about what they wanted to be. A concert hall wanted to be a violin in a violin case.

I think that David Rockwell has conversations with the ideas of his buildings because some of his designs look as he talks. I feel they do. I hear my version of places talking within them.

Rockwell Group's design of Nobu, a restaurant in New York City, seems like a conversation with chopsticks, stones, and the unique food that represents Japan itself.

The new building for Oscar is an extravaganza celebrating what people whisper to each other during the ceremony: "There is so-and-so," "Look what so-and-so is wearing," "He should win," "They are smaller than I thought," "She is less (or more) beautiful than I thought." It celebrates the swooning that happens during the processional that is the Oscars. This building creates and gives rise to the conversations that make up the memory of the event itself.

David Rockwell's architecture is about the conversations we have with each other, with ourselves, and with what a building wants to be.

When an architect or designer touches on a simple truth, he or she knows what he or she wants to do as opposed to how to do it. What is the primal creative ideation? There are many hows, but only one what.

Years ago, I started a series of guidebooks based on the conversations I had with cities. My main question was "Where am I and what is around me?" This question created the Access Guides. A question, a phrase, even a word can begin a building.

The Bible starts with "In the beginning there was the word."

The first line to the introduction to my book on Lou Kahn stated, "He was the youngest person I ever knew." I think David Rockwell epitomizes that spirit in so many of his projects.

Projects that shelter events, sports, and hospitality are the vocabulary of wonder and youth. Stadia, restaurants, and hotels form the alphabet of clients of his work.

Next time you go in or walk by one of David Rockwell's many creations, listen to what it is saying to you and talk back.

Richard Saul Wurman is the author and designer of eighty books, the recipient of numerous grants and design awards, the creator of the TED (Technology/Entertainment/Design) conferences and the Access Guides. Wurman was trained as an architect at the University of Pennsylvania.

155

ent

There is a fascination these days with big buildings. Just ask Rem Koolhaas, who outlined his obsession with largeness in his hefty treatise, *S,M,L,XL.* Architects and theorists like Koolhaas seem mesmerized by megaplexes, convention centers, airports, outlet malls, and stadiums, enthralled with their vastness, regardless of whether or not bigger buildings are any more interesting than tiny jewels.

Add to that list Mohegan Sun, the Mohegan tribe's vast gaming and entertainment complex in eastern Connecticut. Everything about Mohegan Sun, especially its recent expansion, is big. Weighing in at four million square feet, phase II comprises a casino, a convention center, an arena with 10,000 seats, a cabaret, 200,000 square feet of shops, and a 1,200-room hotel (designed by Kohn Pedersen Fox Associates). There are 12 restaurants, 5 lounges, a nightclub, 80 gaming tables, and 2,600 slot machines. There are acres of terrazzo, a dozen custom carpet patterns, a crystalline rock made of twelve thousand pieces of onyx, and colorful canopies woven from thirty million glass beads, each weighing two tons. Fueling so much bigness is big money: The newest phase alone cost $1 billion—as much as Richard Meier's much vaunted Getty Center in L.A.— and the entire complex brings in a profit measured in the hundreds of millions each year.

Bigger certainly isn't inherently better for a firm like Rockwell Group, who excel at crafting joyful experiences at the more intimate scale of restaurants, hotels, and the stage. (Not that the firm hasn't already designed larger projects with equal aplomb.) Yet this was the firm who designed the first phase of Mohegan Sun and who was later asked to more than double the size of their original creation. How could any designer make sense of such an ambitious expansion, a space so vast that your jaw would drop just to see it empty? How could any architect sustain people's interest as they navigate through millions of square feet of space and keep a smile on their face all the while?

For Rockwell Group, the answer came, as it often does, from theater, where David Rockwell himself has deep roots. (He did stage lighting early in his career and more recently created sets for a Broadway version of *The Rocky Horror Show* and a stage production of the cult-classic John Waters film, *Hairspray.*) To start making

sense of the immense program of the expanded Mohegan Sun, he borrowed a page from set design and made Mohegan Sun a colossal, inhabitable stage set within a vast box. The result is an epic scenographic landscape worthy of Cinecittá or baroque Rome.

For Rockwell, the starting point of any engaging stage set is the weaving together of individually static pieces into a dynamic whole. It's the combination of grand and intimate gestures, the expected and unexpected that make theatrical spaces so, well, theatrical. Orchestrating phase II's immense interior into a compelling, comprehensible whole began with the program, which involves much more than just gambling. Visitors can shop, have lunch, shop some more, get a massage, have dinner, hear a concert, sip a nightcap, and check in for the night—and do it all again the next day. Rockwell Group collaged the distinct-but-related functions of commerce, casino, and entertainment, breaking down the programmatic divisions one might find in a run-of-the-mill Vegas casino. By placing stores, restaurants, entertainment venues, and slot machines in close proximity, the plan energizes the "bounce" (in mall-developer lingo) between functions and encourages visitors to continually discover new spaces. Shopping, eating, and gambling become interrelated activities. The net effect is a much more dynamic spatial environment than phase I, whose Casino of the Earth is a static ring of gaming areas surrounding a circular lounge and theater known as the Wolf Den, with restaurants beyond the outer ring of slot machines and game tables.

The choreography of movement that draws visitors through the sprawling set has as much to do with a variety of differently scaled spaces as with the diversity of functions. None of the spaces qualifies as small, but relative differences among different areas help break down the scale of the vast interior into smaller, more understandable pieces, and help users navigate their way through the building.

Ordinarily, easy wayfinding is the mark of good design; but in the gaming world, it's taboo. Casino design aims to lure gamblers in and disorient them, so they spend more time—and money—while lost in a labyrinth. Rather than disorienting visitors, Rockwell actually helped them

navigate through vast, windowless interiors—just one of the many casino-industry standards that Rockwell Group broke with in their design.

In the Casino of the Earth, Rockwell marked the four cardinal points within the circular plan and designed each around one of the four seasons. The lashed timber "trees" have grids of cutout acrylic leaves that reveal the seasons through color, from an icy winter white to bright summertime green. In the Casino of the Sky, Wombi Rock is the luminous landmark around which all the gaming areas and lounges are arranged—and it's a pretty memorable locale. The rock is a three-story outcropping of glowing onyx that speaks to the importance of crystals and mountains in Mohegan lore. Above the rock is the drum of the night sky, rendered in fiber-optic pinpoints of light; inside are a high-roller lounge, a nightclub, and a two-level bar. Smaller planetarium domes mark cross-axes in the winding, circular casino. Following the sun's daily path from east to west, the planetarium at the eastern end of the casino displays the morning stars, while the dome at the western end contains the stars you'd see as the sun set. At the convergence of the hotel lobby, shopping arcade, and casino, a huge waterfall, the Taughannick Falls, creates a memorable orientation point.

The typical casino offers no clues to the outside world. It's an inwardly focused otherworld of suspended belief, where you're looking to get lost in the game. There are no windows, no clocks, and no easy way out. At Mohegan Sun there are—gasp—huge skylights. They may not give clear indications of the time of day or even the weather, but they bring precious natural light into the cavernous interiors, reminding gamblers, however subtly, of life on the outside. Curiously, everything inside suggests the outside: rocks, waterfalls, rain, an allée of trees, the sheltering, starlit planetarium skies. This is the ultimate reversal of casino fantasy, a transporting world based not on historical settings or distant destinations, but on nature.

Even the ceiling heights, measuring forty-five feet, break with convention. The increased height allows towering structures and spaces to be built beneath them, and creates far more exhilarating spaces than the low, dark warrens typical of most casinos. It seems logical to the outside observer, but Rockwell's unorthodox strategy—for the casino world, at least—pays off. When they're energized and entranced by an evocatively designed space, you don't need winding mazes, total darkness, and low ceilings to keep the crowds gambling; they linger of their own will because they enjoy the space.

Like any good stage set, the scenography of Mohegan Sun supports the telling of a story without dominating the tale. In this case, the set pieces spin allegorical narratives from the Mohegan tribe's long tradition of storytelling. (At the start of the design process, tribal leaders gave Rockwell Group a 300-page design brief filled with in-depth discussions of the many symbols of Mohegan culture.) Just about every element of Mohegan Sun is imbued with symbolism, from Wombi Rock to the carpet patterns and door pulls; nothing is accidental or superfluous. The curving footprint of the retail corridor refers to the Mohegans' marking of time and commemorating events with a "life trail," while the surface of the path itself—carpets describing deserts, mountains, and water through color and pattern—outlines the tribe's nomadic wanderings throughout its history. The giant tortoise-shell dome represents a mythical turtle on whose back the Mohegans believed the earth was lifted out of water. Even the tiny stars depicted in the casino's four mini-planetariums tell of constellations of significance to the tribe.

In the original Casino of the Earth, Rockwell Group created a literal-minded language of leather-lashed

timbers reminiscent of traditional Mohegan structures, dry-stacked stone walls, and even fake wolves to convey tribal symbolism. In phase II, the designers abstracted that symbolism without diminishing its relevance. This new abstract vocabulary is even more powerful than its predecessor, because it's more concerned with evoking emotion than communicating specific references. If you don't understand the significance to the Mohegans of crystals, trees, or stars, the impact of the device is not diminished. In fact, many Mohegan symbols have multiple meanings often based on similitude. For example, the thirteen subdivisions of a tortoiseshell relate to the thirteen moons of a calendar year; the roots of a tree (that grow from a turtle's back) link the earth and the sky in the Mohegan genesis story. Regardless of your literacy in native symbolism, you are moved by the craftsmanship of the pieces, stirred by the colors and lights, impressed by their size, and ultimately delighted by them. What counts more than the legibility of the symbols is the experience of being sheltered beneath an opalescent dome or wandering beneath a sparkling canopy of color and light. These are sensations anyone can enjoy; and that universal appeal is a central tenet of the Rockwell Group philosophy.

Ironically, the more abstract language of phase II conveys a greater sense of craft and materiality than phase I's literal evocations of lashed timbers and woven wood. Even from three stories below, the handmade quality of the sparkling, brilliantly colored glass-bead canopies above the artificial "trees" of the retail corridor is palpable. In the restaurant Rain, metal-leafed marbles set into walls of plaster behind flowing water make the water look and feel even wetter, if such a thing is possible. Woven wood panels above the storefronts of the retail concourse and woven copper and brass on the hotel check-in desk nod to the Mohegans' weaving traditions in their handicrafts. Even Wombi Rock has a hand-built quality, even though it's meant to evoke a natural geological formation.

Sometimes you can touch these materials; often you can't. But even when touch is not allowed, the tactile quality comes across visually. Just by looking at them, you can imagine what it would feel like to run your fingers across the woven wood, the glass beads, or the metallic marbles.

That tangible, handmade quality—a signature of Rockwell Group's work, though one that has rarely been applied at such an enormous scale—is part of the firm's appeal to all the senses. The strategy helps keep visitors tuned in and turned on as they wander through the sprawling complex. The overwhelmingly visual nature of the design is its most obvious feature. In the restaurant Rain, it literally rains down along the plaster walls. Water also flows from the hotel lobby down an artificial cascade of Taughannick

Falls, in front of which a kinetic glass sculpture by Dale Chihuly erupts like a geyser from a wooden bridge.

Other senses aren't ignored. In most casinos, the only sound you hear is the din of ringing, coin-spouting slot machines; but at Mohegan Sun, the waterfall generates a loud rush of water that masks some of the clamor. Wombi Rock, surprisingly, provides an oasis of quiet even in the midst of the casino commotion. As for taste, dozens of restaurants please the palate. Many of them also appeal to the sense of smell with open kitchens; Tuscany, a restaurant located at the base of the waterfall, even boasts an open barbeque pit that sends sizzling sounds and aromas wafting into the casino.

As in any theatrical event, all things lead to a show-stopping climax—what's been called "the big wow" in other Rockwell Group projects, or what might vulgarly be called "the money shot" in cinematic lingo. In phase II, the show-stopper is Wombi Rock. Of course, there can be no grand finale without a buildup. The supporting spaces that make Wombi Rock such a knockout are smaller variations on the theme of the sky-dome: a tightly woven, nearly Baroque promenade of four smaller planetarium drums and the faceted "tortoiseshell" dome. The whole of phase II presents variations on Wombi Rock's glow and transparency, with elements of translucency and sparkle.

If ever Rockwell Group was unsure its usual magic could work in so immense a space as Mohegan Sun, they can rest easy now: It has. They've turned what could have been another vast, soulless casino into a human-scaled spectacle of texture, transparency, and activity, rewriting the rules of casino design in the process. Sometimes, the spectacle seems to last forever—is there no end in sight to this building, you wonder—but for the client, bigness is the name of the game. For Rockwell, the project has given him confidence that emotion can hold sway in a large project, that big spaces need not be anonymous. And that bodes well for all of us who populate large spaces, whether or not we're seduced by bigness.

Raul A. Barreneche is a New York–based architectural critic and writer. He is a contributing editor to Architecture, Metropolitan Home, *and* Travel + Leisure *magazines, and has also written for* Dwell, Interior Design, Wallpaper, *and the* New York Times, *among other publications. He is coauthor of* House: American Houses for the New Century *(Universe, 2001) and is currently at work on a new book about residential architecture around the world.*

159

du soleil

A focal point for Walt Disney World Resort's new Downtown Disney West Side Entertainment District, the Cirque du Soleil building is the Montreal-based company's first freestanding home. Using model-massing and form-finding programs developed by the auto industry, Rockwell Group combined a tensile structure with a conventional building mass. The exterior "fabric," made from Teflon-coated fiberglass, soars to 160 feet and echoes Cirque's traveling show tent. The drumlike structure within was inspired by simple volumes of industrial architecture, such as water towers and gas tanks. Technical challenges facing the project included an extremely high water table and the requirement that the construction be able to withstand hurricane-force winds. Rooted to solid foundations and almost stretching to the ground in some spots, visitors can touch the building's fiberglass skin. Under these white folds, an outdoor platform allows entertainers to perform before the show, offering a preview of the dynamic and colorful space within. Abstracted jester's hats and patterns inspired by Picasso's *Harlequin* fill the lobby and set the tone for the performance to come.

1 theater interior
2 cirque, at dusk
3 exploded axonometric with plan
4 top of stairs at entry
5 masting
6 detail of mast
7 at night from lagoon

Performing Arts Space
Orlando, Florida
1999

163

2

65

3 4

Box Office

5 | 6

7

The goal of the master plan for Complexe Cirque in Hong Kong would be to "engineer" a stage for cultural, educational, and entertainment activities using landscape rather than architecture. Two principal challenges were addressed by this approach. One was the desire to create a defined and identifiable district within Kowloon, where art and culture would be accessible and tangible. The second was to provide an ambitious and organic infrastructure to accommodate different uses such as performing centers, water markets, hotels, spas, and museums without compromising the area's complex urban infrastructure. In collaboration with Michel Crête, Claude Cormier, and Johnny Boivin (as well as Elizabeth Diller and Ricardo Scofidio for the hotel and spa), Rockwell Group intended to create an undulating landscape that organically connects the city and the harbor. Because the surrounding buildings are tall, the 1.2-million-square-foot district establishes its identity by means of horizontality, achieved in part through the continuity of the "urban carpet."

1 cirque theater and water market
2 aerial overview
3 glowing landscape
4 night district
5 housing district
6 main plaza
7 artists' housing overview
8 spa overview

Master Plan
Hong Kong
2001

complexe cirque

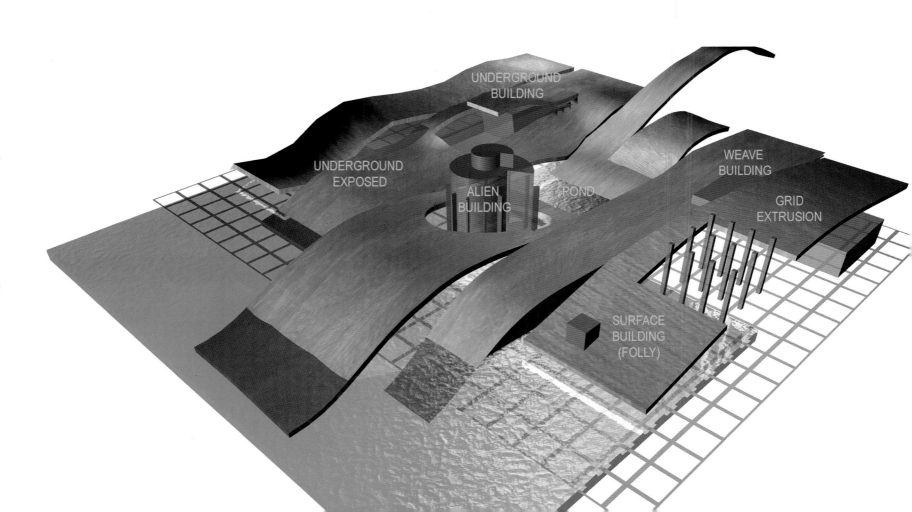

UNDERGROUND BUILDING

UNDERGROUND EXPOSED

ALIEN BUILDING

POND

WEAVE BUILDING

GRID EXTRUSION

SURFACE BUILDING (FOLLY)

169

complexe cirque

171

koo

kodak thea

1

Kodak Theatre is the new home for the annual Academy Awards presentation. It is a unique venue designed both for the technical demands of broadcast television and live music, dance, and theater performances. The architects studied movie palaces of the 1920s, whose immersive environments were known at the time as "atmospheric theaters." The phrase "The show starts at the sidewalk" was coined to describe the notion that the interior experience could begin to resonate at the exterior; this idea became the rationale for the giant curtain at the Hollywood Boulevard entrance of the Kodak Theatre. As the theater itself is set back from Hollywood Boulevard, a public galleria, the "Awards Walk" provides an elegant procession from the boulevard to the theater. The Awards Walk is characterized by a series of limestone portals with backlit glass panels celebrating the Best Picture winners from 1927/28 through the year 2074. Inside, the theater achieves a surprising intimacy through the use of box seating along the sides of the house, inspired by European opera houses, as well as carefully raked seating at the main level and each of the three balconies. In addition, the distinctive "Tiara" ceiling structure, a swirling silver-leafed lattice, extends downward through the opera box ensemble to unify the entire volume. The balcony fronts are further defined by backlit, cast glass panels. The 180,000-square-foot theater seats 3,300 for Oscars night, but by closing its upper balcony, it can transform into a 2,700-seat theater, more appropriate for touring shows.

1 entry portal and "red carpet" corridor
2 lobby stair and circulation
3 house seating, boxes, stage, with tiara ceiling

Performing Arts Space
Hollywood, California
2001

175

kodak theatre

173

theater

rocky horror

For the stage revival of the cult-classic *The Rocky Horror Show,* not seen in New York for a quarter of a century, Rockwell Group sought to capture the energy of a rock-and-roll show with the quirky fun of a midnight showing of the cult movie. Working with the stylistic influences of 1950s horror and sci-fi B movies, the design creates a contemporary version of that world. Within the confines of a small theater with limited sight lines, Rockwell Group concentrated on harnessing the power of the juxtapositions created by unexpected set transformations, as well as creating an environment that envelops the audience. Described as "strikingly fluid" and "eye-popping," all aspects of the theater engage the viewer. The lobby is shrink-wrapped in Gothic red and festooned with

mannequins; on the stage itself, the movie screen prosceniums disappear and a "movie theater within a theater" vanishes in a dramatic sweep as the floor flips over with its movie seats and "patrons" intact, bringing them into the distorted and bizarre world of Frank 'n' Furter. The set design of *The Rocky Horror Show* was nominated for a Drama Desk Award in 2001.

1 frank 'n' furter's laboratory
2 wrapped body concept
3 contact sheet of scene-by-scene

Set Design
Circle in the Square Theatre
New York City
2000

181

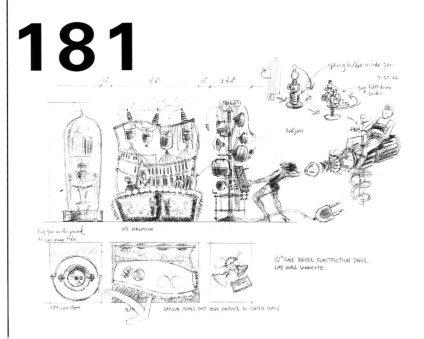

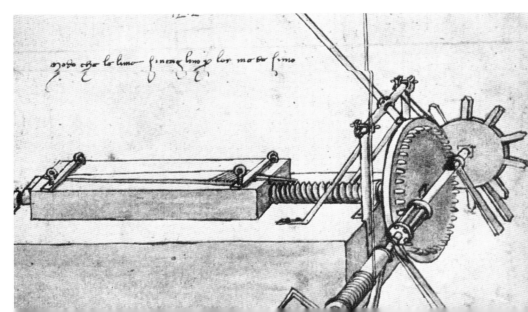

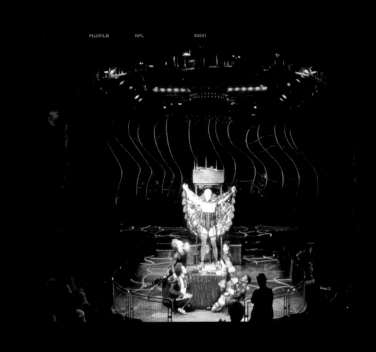

Challenged with helping turn the 1988 movie *Hairspray* into a new Broadway production, Rockwell Group's goal was to capture the unexpected and quirky humor of the original John Waters' film in a theatrical setting. Staged as a musical, *Hairspray* follows the teenage Tracy Turnblad in her quest to land a spot on a dance show at the local TV station in her hometown of Baltimore. The story, set in 1962, addresses social issues on a small and larger scale: the timeless torture of being a chubby teenager who doesn't fit in, as well as the contemporary debate on integration. Playing with the idea of flattened surface appearance created by television, Rockwell Group used graphic patterns and abstracted forms for the set design. Creating obviously two-dimensional scenery, the designers subvert the ideas of realism and perspective traditionally used in set design. The city of Baltimore is represented with schematic row houses and their signature formstone facades. The scenery for the TV station, in which much of the action takes place, suggests the flatness of early TV shows and features a backdrop of wide vertical stripes in pastel hues, inspired by Necco Wafers. A latticework of microphone booms drops from above, adding a behind-the-scenes dimension of a working TV studio. This type of visual layering is used throughout the production to create a variety of spatial effects. A contour curtain made of plastic red tubing and blue velour that turns into an enormous hairdo with a barette and an LED wall with 610 circular pegs evoking a Lite Brite toy are other visual highlights of the show.

1 finale with hair curtain

Set Design
Neil Simon Theater
New York City
2002

hairspray

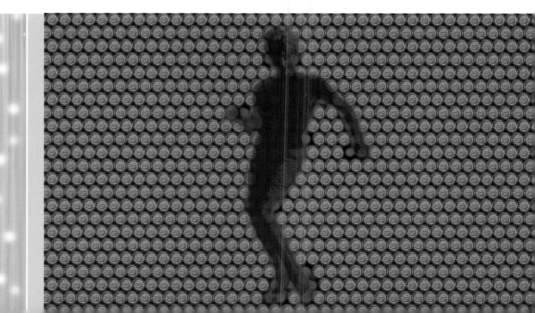

185

sports

skyfield

BATTER UP

1

2 3

A collaboration between the Coca-Cola Company and the Atlanta Braves, Skyfield is a 22,000-square-foot rooftop plaza/park overlooking left field at Atlanta's Turner Field. Intended as a recreational environment that both enhances and supplements the baseball experience, Skyfield is a family-oriented space. Its surface grass features a miniature "baseball field" that allows spectators to participate in the game. In addition, a full-scale replica of the base path from home plate to first base is a simple device that engages fans. Rockwell Group's concept fuses the imagery and memories of the Atlanta Braves with Coca-Cola. Large, stylized baseball card banners ring the Skyfield and can be seen from the interstate as well as from inside the stadium. A giant Coca-Cola bottle was

created using actual Major League Baseball gear, such as home plates, baseballs, bats, and Braves memorabilia. An active piece of sculpture, the bottle shoots fireworks out of the top whenever an Atlanta Brave hits a home run.

1 coke bottle and firework cannon
2 memorabilia detail of coke bottle
3 giant baseball cards, fan
  experience area

Stadium
Atlanta
1997

189

It's the real thing.
Coke.

Comerica Park is a synthesis of tradition and theater, celebrating the team heritage of the Detroit Tigers in monumental yet playful terms. The time-honored architectural vocabulary of baseball's great stadiums is the foundation here. The twenty-two-acre site is fully integrated with the surrounding community through scale, materials, and regional decorative motifs made by local craftsmen. What makes Comerica Park unique, however, is the focus on guest participation and involvement. Restaurants, retail stores, a Big-Cat food court, a baseball Ferris wheel, and a tiger carousel within the park make it a vibrant destination for local residents and baseball fans. There are also post- and pregame opportunities for fans, including photographs with majestic, snarling tigers at the entrance, or by columns that are fluted with "scratches" from the enormous tiger paws. Fans can also have their picture taken next to the towering baseball bats that make up the entrance gate—large-scale versions of bats used by Tiger legends Ty Cobb, Hank Greenberg, and Al Kaline. The concourses turn into museums of Tiger history with displays of artifacts and memorabilia collected since the team's inception in the nineteenth century.

1 tiger sculpture detail, main
  ballpark entry
2 main ballpark entry
3 entry gates

Stadium
Detroit
2000

comerica park

IRECTOR GRIFFITH WOULD BUILD A $500,000 IMPROVEMENT FOR THE DETROIT MUSEUM OF

191

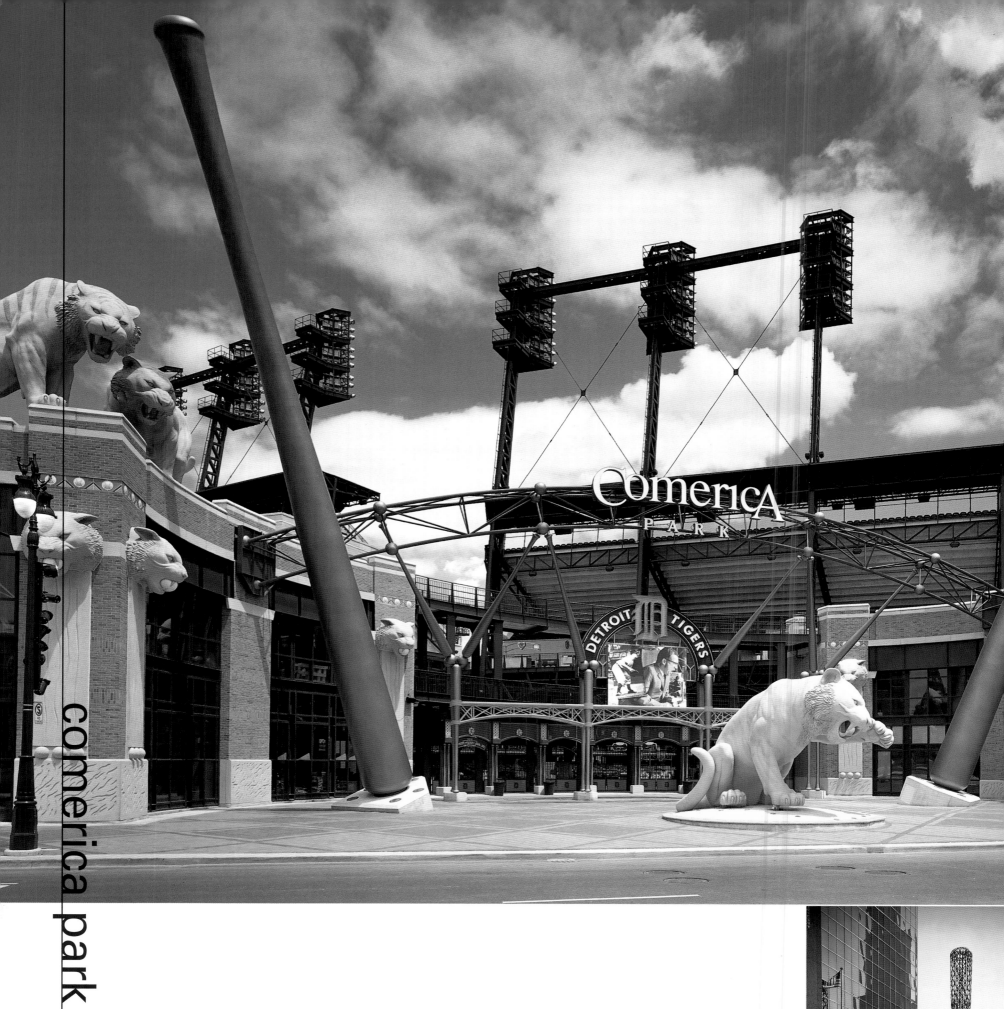

comerica park

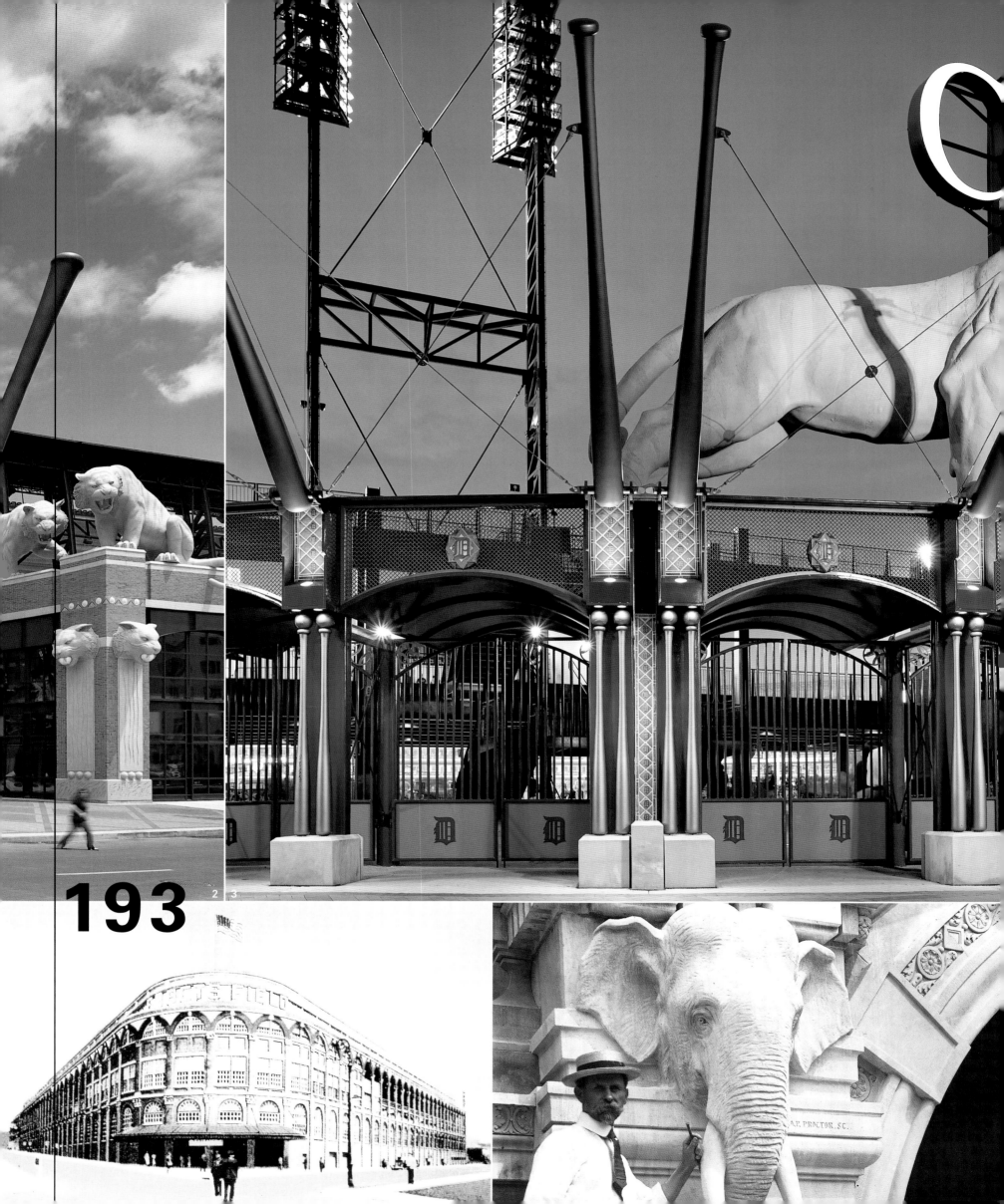

193

2 3

For the site of the West Side Rail Yard in Manhattan, Rockwell Group developed an urban plan that would expand the Jacob Javits Center while at the same time creating a new home for New York City's sports teams. Working with Madison Square Garden and the New York Jets, Rockwell Group designed arenas with the city's professional football, hockey, and basketball teams in mind. Envisioned as a sports megalopolis, the Fantasy Sports Complex project covers one urban block (over twenty acres) and rises to a height of sixty stories. The sports arenas are on a scale that would accommodate the Olympic Games, putting New York into the running as a future host city. In addition to a super stadium with transforming National Football League (80,000-plus seating)

and Olympic (100,000 seats) capacity, the building includes the Madison Sky Garden area for basketball and hockey (20,000-plus seating) and franchise player penthouses. A thousand-room, twenty-story U-shaped hotel sits atop this sports universe. Part of the site would also include retail and other types of entertainment venues, such as the two-thousand-seat Cirque du Soleil Theater.

Rockwell Group's Master Plan for the National Football League's largest venue, the Coliseum at Exposition Park in Los Angeles, would allow football fans and park enthusiasts to share a common space. The new design would retain the existing L.A. Coliseum's exterior walls and its landmark peristyle. The peristyle would be

penetrated by a park, allowing the public to engage with the Coliseum. The plan includes fifty acres of park on top of an underground parking system, which would accommodate the parking needed for the stadium, while also giving acres of outdoor space back to the community. Inside the 72,500-seat stadium, the luxury boxes are designed to reflect everyday life in Los Angeles, with small "lawns" and trellises for shading.

1 stacked stadium rendering, fantasy sports complex
2 master plan rendering, coliseum at exposition park

Arena and Stadium, Stadium
New York City, Los Angeles
2000, 1999

fantasy complex

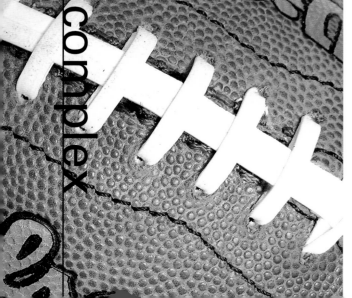

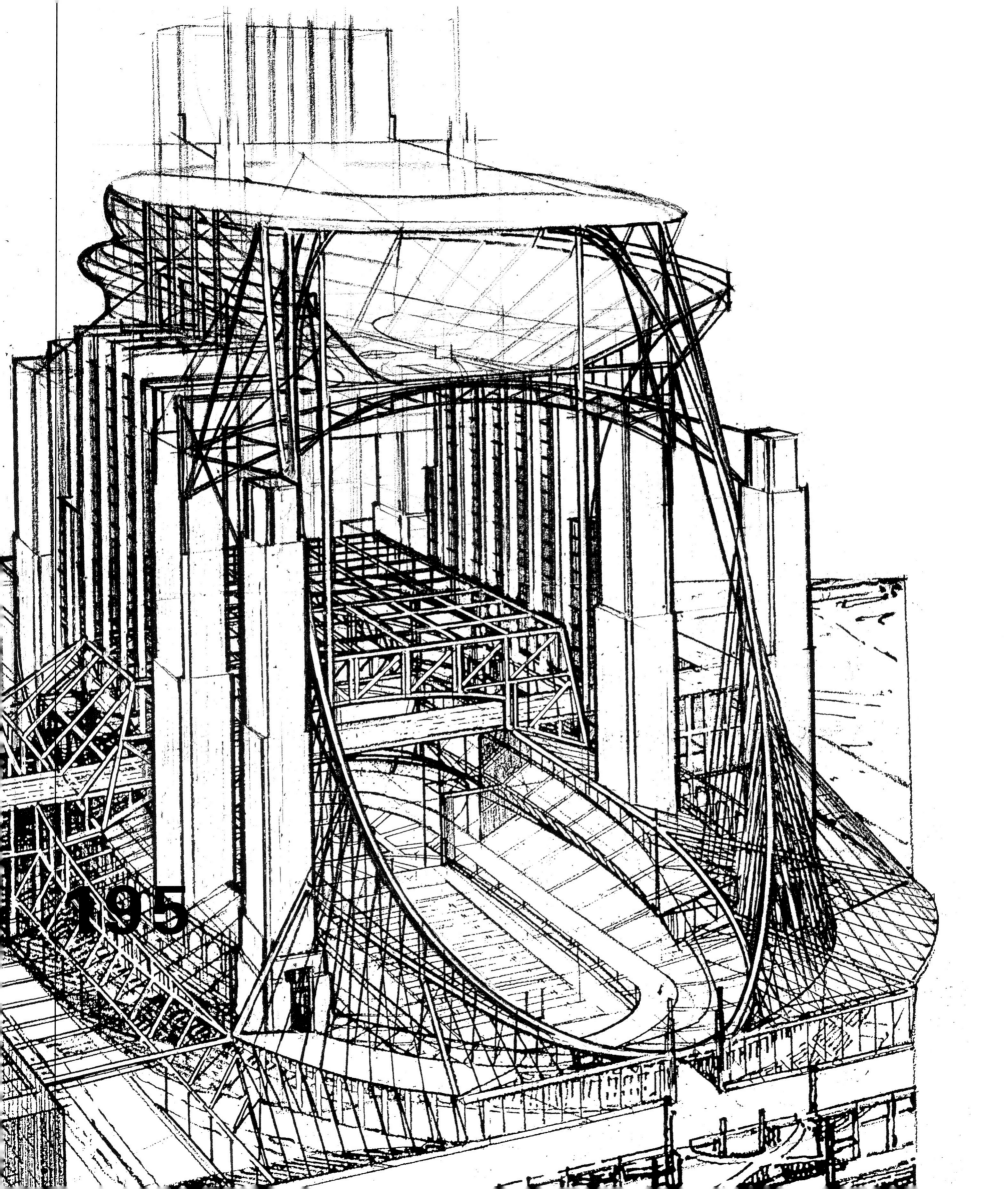

coliseum

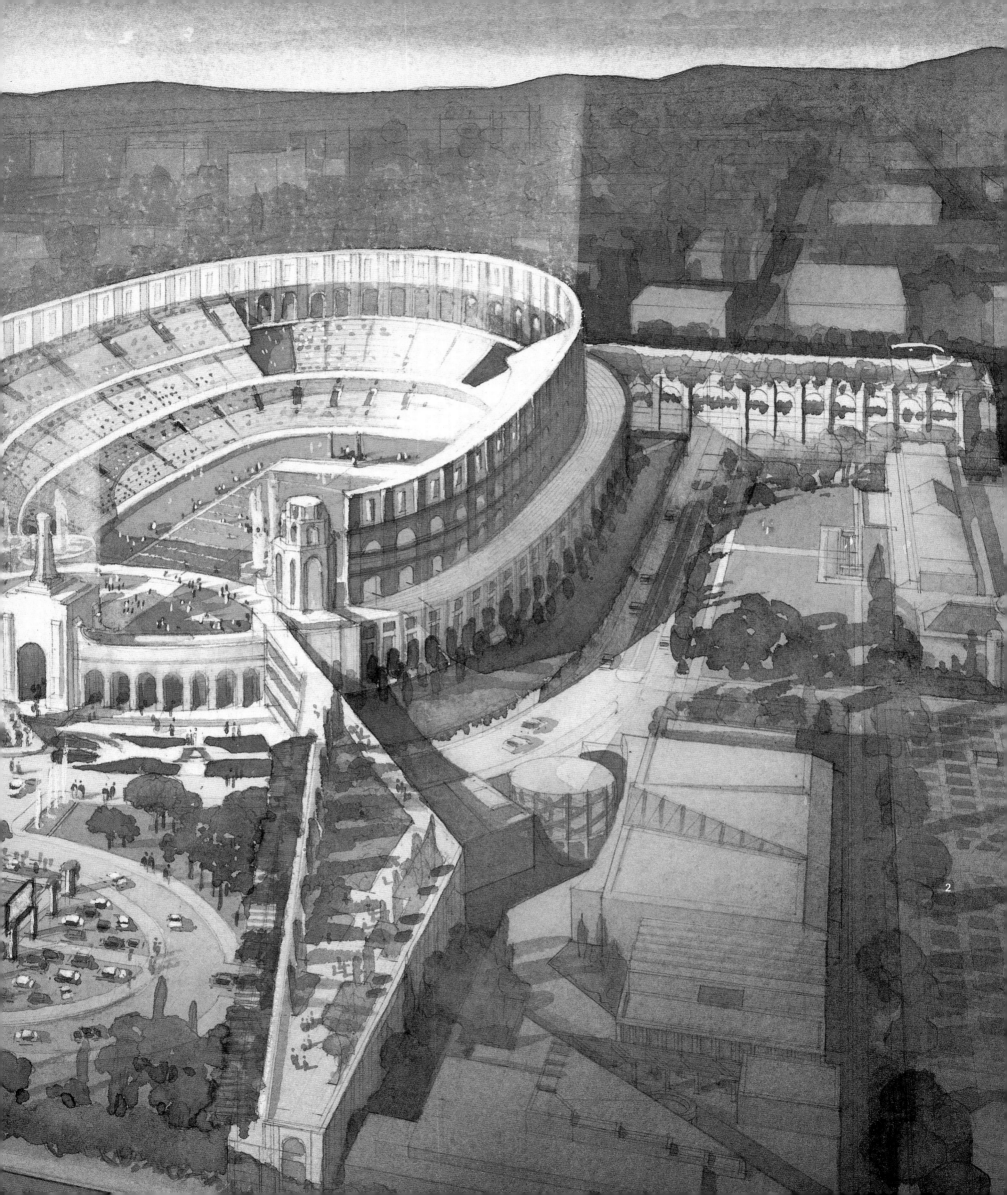

2

hegan sun

mohegan earth

The Mohegan Sun project, located in Uncasville, Connecticut, is on the site of the ancestral home of the Native American Mohegan tribe. For Rockwell Group, the challenge was to create an immersive entertainment experience by incorporating symbolic elements of the history and mythology of the Mohegan tribe, which, at one time, was close to extinction. Working alongside an existing 200,000-square-foot building, Rockwell Group's design adds 300,000 square feet of space that is organized by a circular walkway and divided into four quadrants relating to the four seasons in Mohegan culture. Unlike traditional casinos, natural light is allowed in through skylights, ceilings are high, and gaming tables and slot machines are integrated into the overall design. At the center is the Wolf Den,

an open performance venue. Rather than literally re-create traditional Mohegan structures or artifacts, Rockwell Group created an architectural vocabulary that references traditional construction methods and uses rustic materials to give form to the tribe's rich oral history. The experience is a visual narrative that envelops the visitor in Mohegan culture. Traditional Mohegan decorative designs and patterns, such as the circle of four quadrants, the "life-trail," and important natural motifs such as trees, are woven into the visual tapestry of the scenographic landscape. The design creates an architecture of hyperdensity and collage that is experienced as though it were a cinema.

Serving as a gateway for Mohegan Sun is the Mohegan Fueling Facility, perched on a hill overlooking the Thames River. The design interprets motifs from inside the casino in a more modern way, creating a space that is functional but in keeping with the character of the resort's overall look. Inside, one wall is set with colored glass gems. The coffee shop is shaped like a nautilus, and topped by a circular, multicolored "lantern." A seventy-five-foot tower capped by a torchère serves as a signpost for the site. I.D. Magazine Annual Design Awards honored Mohegan Sun, Casino of the Earth in 1997. This project was designed in association with Brennan Beer Gorman / Architects.

1 tower beacon, fueling facility
2 porte cochere, east entry
3 spring entry
4 trellis work detail, summer entry
5 winter casino
6 basket weave detail, longhouse restaurant
7 winter entry
8 log and leather lashing
9 glass storefront, fueling facility
10 fueling facility

Casino and Fueling Facility
Uncasville, Connecticut
1996–2002

201

mohegan earth

203

3 4

5 6

mohegan earth

"It is as ambitiou
of stagecraft as
realized since th
Cecil B. DeMille."

Herbert Muschamp on Mohegan Earth, *New York Times,* October 21, 1996

Fueled by the success of its 1996 casino, the Mohegan Sovereign Nation, the developers of Mohegan Sun, Casino of the Earth, proposed an expansion intended to transform their existing facility into a holiday destination. The project consists of a four-million-square-foot addition that includes a second casino, a thousand-room hotel (designed by Kohn Pedersen Fox Associates PC), a convention center, a 10,000-seat arena, and a 300,000-square-foot retail and entertainment facility. In planning the public spaces of the expansion, Rockwell Group extended the clarity and ease of orientation in the existing facility, building upon the visual language that was developed in the first casino. Once again, the design is based on narrative drawn from the tribe's oral history; for

example, the migration of the tribe is evoked in the iconography of the retail corridor that connects the two casinos. References to traditional Mohegan crafts are incorporated into the architecture through the use of woven wood and glass beads. The literal architectural vocabulary of the Casino of the Earth is transformed into a more abstract vocabulary in the Casino of the Sky. There, a massive crystalline formation of glowing onyx, Wombi Rock, alludes to the crystals once found on the tribe's site; it also refers to the rock formations where the Mohegan leaders traditionally met their councilors. Wombi Rock is situated below a 150-foot-diameter planetarium and organized on three levels, housing a nightclub, bar, and lounge.

1 taughannick falls from hotel lobby
2 retail corridor with memory pile
  in foreground
3 beaded canopy details
4 tree of life, retail corridor
5 wombi rock lounge
6 turtleback lounge
7 gaming floor from wombi peak
8 sacred cedar grove, hotel lobby

Casino and Resort
Uncasville, Connecticut
1999–2002

mohegan sky

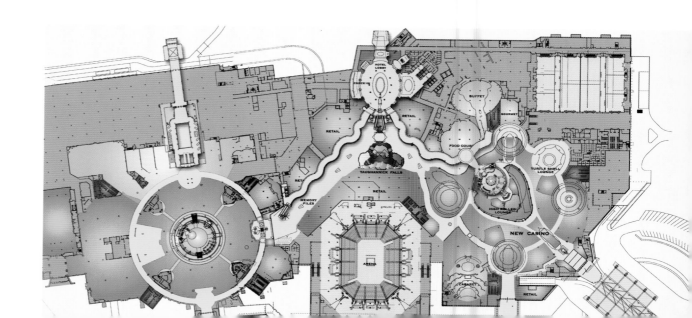

211

mohegan sky

2 3

213

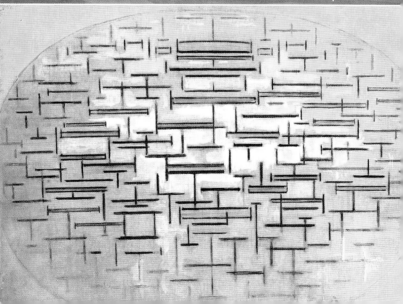

mohegan sky

mohegan

7

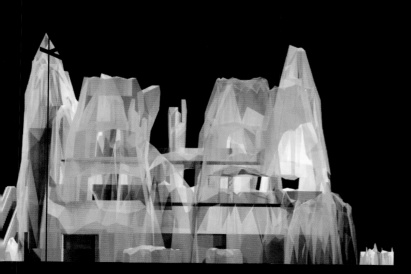

217

THE MAKING GENE
TODD OLDHAM

There are many schools of thought concerning the origins of creativity. Could it indeed be some sort of communal consciousness, or perhaps a result of our overstimulation by electronic media? It's hard to define, but I imagine that if we were to look for the origin of the need to make, we would find it nestled in our DNA. In which case, a look into the DNA of David Rockwell and his team at Rockwell Group would tell us that they possess at least double the amount of the "making gene," or "MG," that most have. After all, Rockwell Group does display all the signs of having advanced MG. Witness their choice of wall coverings for the exotic sushi restaurant Next Door Nobu in New York. In a bold tribute to what's on the menu, Rockwell Group swathed the walls in yards (er . . . pounds?) of Noori seaweed, resulting in a richly hued iridescent surface that could never have been obtained using paint.

Those, like Rockwell Group, with advanced MG are often accused of bothering to bother. For instance, at Mohegan Sun casino in Connecticut Rockwell Group wanted to create a ceiling as rich in color and texture as the Native American bead crafts from which it was inspired. For a project that could be measured in acres, it would have been simple to hire scenic painters or apply photographic murals, but Rockwell Group knew that nothing would be as beautiful as swirling ceiling murals executed entirely by hand using small glass beads.

Often, a bracketless view of possibilities and the knowledge that nearly everything can be recycled leads those with MG to some odd successes. In the strangely elegant Mexican restaurant Rosa Mexicano in New York, diners feast on what might be the world's best guacamole while sitting in chairs made from used car seatbelt straps. No one would suspect that the warm ochres, rusts, and plum shades of the chairs share as much with the beautiful colors of Mexico as they do with the Ford Pintos and AMC Gremlins from our recent past. In homage to the cliff divers of Acapulco, Rockwell Group created an indoor waterfall that cascades down two stories of handmade cobalt blue glass tiles. Intrigued by the graceful positions of the divers themselves, they made and attached to the waterfall an army of hundreds of twelve-inch divers positioned as if in mid-dive, their white clay toes just skimming the surface of the falling water.

Rockwell Group's advanced MG shined particularly bright when they took on Broadway in 2001 for the restaging of the beloved *Rocky Horror Show* at Circle in the Square Theatre. A notorious design challenge, the theater was completely transformed with Rockwell charm. I can just hear David Rockwell easily convincing the cast to make their entrances perched atop chandeliers that would be designed to descend from the theater's upper level to the stage floor, and to hang like bugs upside down on sinewy metal grids for entire dance numbers. The whole show was a dazzling display of moving ingenuity culminating in a wild transformation from a spooky old castle to an RKO theater in mere seconds by flipping floors and crumbling sets that reassembled right in front of our eyes.

For the furniture at the cozily futuristic restaurant Pod in Philadelphia, Rockwell Group turned to some very unusual resources. Clearly understanding the thrill of the ride, they went right to the source, working with a company that manufactures roller-coaster cars for amusement parks. Diners at Pod sit atop squishy booths that have been dipped like petit fours in a seamless, bright-colored rubber that, when sat upon, molds perfectly to the body's contours. What better material for restaurant seating than amusement park–strength rubber?

While the debate on the origins of MG will no doubt continue, we can all be grateful for one truth: a glorious entity like Rockwell Group, who are endlessly inspired and hired to design everything around us, is percolating with the stuff.

Todd Oldham, principal of Todd Oldham Studio in New York City, is a celebrated interior designer and photographer, and an award-winning designer of men's and women's fashions.

SPACE
GEORGE C. WOLFE

When one works in theater, regardless of the scale of the project or how humble or grand its ambitions, it almost always invariably ends up invading one's life, requiring more space than was initially anticipated. Like some 1950s science-fiction creature, it benignly enters your being, asking only to access your imagination. And yet by project's end, it has consumed one's entire existence, parasitically demanding more time, blood, and energy than one has for one's self.

When you work on a project, a piece of you dies with its birth and is forever sacrificed and offered up to the collective energy and memory for all those who worked on or witnessed the production. And so when one begins to discuss any aspect of a theater project, I find it impossible to speak only from the vantage point of how the play is ultimately embodied. The final script of *Angels in America* is full of the exhaustion and exhilaration of the actors and myself trying to navigate the emotional and intellectual rigor of performing Part One at night, all the while remaining flexible and incorporating Tony Kushner's brilliant daily rewrites during rehearsals for Part Two. Photographic stills from *Bring in 'da Noise, Bring in 'da Funk* reverberate with the exuberant sense of perpetual motion and childlike play which informed and defined the creation of that show.

Theater is more than just the space it occupies. And Rockwell Group's designs for *The Rocky Horror Show* are a brilliant material manifestation of this idea. They occupy more than just the space normally set aside for a production. I firmly believe the emotional and rhythmic event of a play begins the second one enters the theater. This is evidenced at *The Rocky Horror Show* by the Grand Guignol blood-red satin walls, replete with disembodied limbs, that greet one as one descends the escalators into the Circle in the Square Theatre. Inside the theater the set is an old-fashioned movie palace proscenium complete with a bank of seats, the space between actors and audience safe and clearly defined. But almost instantaneously, the movie palace proscenium is fractured, the bank of seats devoured and replaced by outrageous set pieces—slinky, sexy, and oozing with wit—and that safe and definable space between the audience and actors is joyfully violated. And it is in that violation that the true wonder of theater lives.

Rockwell Group's designs for *The Rocky Horror Show* demand that we surrender to, even as we are liberated by, the visual invasion—just as the theater demands its creators surrender. And in both cases it's a matter of space.

George C. Wolfe is the director of the Joseph Papp Public Theater in New York City. An award-winning writer, director, and producer, he is the recipient of two Tony Awards, the Actor's Equity Association Paul Robeson Award, the Society of Stage Directors and Choreographers' Calloway Award, and the Lambda Liberty Award.

219

Dreaming is one of our missions at Rockwell Group, and what a great mission to have! To imagine is our greatest pleasure and something we do in collaboration with an extraordinary group of artists and designers who help us to blur the boundaries between disciplines and ideas. Collaboration, and all the "messiness" that accompanies it, is not only a mantra of Rockwell Group, it is truly part of our DNA.

It is well in evidence at our office on Union Square West in New York. Every inch is occupied with flea market finds, sketches, recycled materials, models, collections of toys, all thrown together in a kind of three-dimensional habitable collage—hardly the pristine studio most people might expect an architect's office to be. I think this controlled chaos clearly reflects the plurality of our interests as well as the diversity of those who work with us. It is home to some ninety designers as well as artists, sculptors, chefs, opera singers, architects, playwrights, and set designers. A bevy of dogs ensures a sense of companionship and that we don't take ourselves too seriously. In short, it's the perfect environment for what we do and what we believe in.

Much of the work represented in this book is experimental: we never tire of trying a new approach even at the risk of tripping up on occasions. In contrast

to design that is consistent in style, our work tends toward a more quirky pluralism. We focus on creating unique design narratives for our projects that inspire their appearance and spirit. The results are frequently eccentric and impolite, and the "messy vitality" that emerges is not altogether surprising given that our inspiration is drawn from cultural landscapes around the globe: pop, new materials, nature, film, and much more.

As a child I fell in love with live theater. Being in an audience and participating in a theatrical experience is one of my greatest pleasures. In theater some of the things that have the most lasting impact are the most fleeting, and so I'm fascinated by how the impact of a performance is embodied in a lasting memory. The relationship between experience and memory, of temporary to permanent, frames much of the work we do. Building and making are immensely fulfilling: It is very seductive to partici-pate in the creation of a place or artifact that is lasting. But I would argue there is something equally seductive about opportunities to experience immediate and momentary pleasures.

Live theater will continue to inspire fresh ideas, as does the theatrical dimension of New York City. The wonderful and unexpected collision of people, places, and events, barely held in equilibrium, affords an immense array of rich experiences. The city both enables and encourages extraordinary diversity: the cacophony of Times Square as it transforms from day to night, the planned and spontaneous aspects of Central Park, the messiness and provisional nature of street fairs and markets. These places have endless potential to excite and entertain, characteristics we strive to engender in our work. As varied as the projects are in appearance, type, and scale, I think they have a common thread: creating the possibilities for pleasure.

COLLABORATORS

From brainstorming sessions with partners to day-to-day teamwork at the office, collaboration is an essential component of Rockwell Group's design process. We want to thank the long-term friends who continue to give us critical input as well as the members of our talented staff.

Walid Abughazaleh, Edward Acero, Carmen Aguilar, Kim Ahkyeong, Jun Aizaki, Blaine Alexander, Louise Allen, Maria Teresa Genoni Alvarez, Carolyn Ament, Jon Angle, Eve Annenberg, Maria Aponte, Jeffrey Appezzato, Timothy Archambault, Robert Ashton, Francis Assaf, Arlene Feldman Avidan, Magdalena Avila

Julius Babalonia, Yael Bahar, Edmond Bakos, Fazlur Baksh, Lisa Baldasare, Claire Baldwin, Bob Bangham, Maria Patricia Barbis, Leonel Barragan, Daniel Barrenechea, Gerald Bartley, Cecelia Behar, Vladimir Belogolovsky, Maria Valerie Ann Benitez, George Bennett, Bridget Benson, Douglas Bergert, Raymond Berrios, Daniela Bertol, Michael Bevilacqua, Michelle Biancardo, Rebeka Bieber, William Bigelow, Ian Birchall, Erich Blohm, Eduardo Bondoc, Joohee Bong, William Bonilla, Ethel Bonn, Jiri Boudnik, Gaylin Bowie, Camilla Bradley, Robert Braun, Oana Bretcanu, Scott Briggs, Michael Brothers, Alexander Brown, Bridget Brown, Kevin Brown, Michael Brown, Susan Brown, Gonzalo Bustamante

Jeannie Campana, Leonard Camposano, David Cantor, Joy Cardillo, Robert Carpenter, Illiam Carrillo, Eduardo Casado, Linda Casper, Jorge Castillo, Vincent Celano, Heather Chamberlain, Cynthia Chan, Eric Chang, Hao Te Chang, Tucker Chauncey, Ramon Chicon, Ryong Hyon Choi, Asiya Chowdhury, Jacquelyne Chu, John Chu, Oswald Chung, Kyle Clark, Luis Clemente-Guzman, Travis Cloud, Natalie Cloutier, Glen Coben, Seth Cohen, Antonio Coke, Katherine Colby, Rosa Maria Colina, Yvonne Colon, Russell Collins, Jack Conviser, Diana Coronato, Anne Corvi, Shirly Corvo, Melanie Cossio-Avallone, Suzanne Couture, Paul Cox, Kevin Coyne, Kathleen Craig, Daniel Cusick

Carl D'Alvia, Claudia Damas, Hilda Daniel, Tushaun Davenport, Roberto De Jesus, Susan De Robertis, Luis

Delance, Guillaume Delemazure, Milagros De Los Santos, Vincent Dell'Aquila, Michael Dereskewicz, Ronald Deschamps, Marc Desmet, Grace Desnoes, Courtney Diefental, Marco Diez, Don Dinkel, Linda Dinkin, Karin Dogny, Alfonso D'Onofrio, Erica Downer, Sara Duffy, Lyman Dunn, Anthony Dunne, Cemre Durusoy

Beverly Eichenlaub, Julia Einspruch, Dawn Ellison, Jose Encarnacion, Nicolas Enista, Eric Epstein, Waleska Erazo, Ragip Erdem

Roger Fairey, Grigori Fateev, Sandi Feinblum, Benn Fennell, Eva Fernandez-Longoria, Frank Festa, Amanda Fin, Michael Fischer, Helena Flecker, Urs Peter Flueckiger, Jason Fox, Krista Fox, Jennifer Fozo, Gabrielle Frahm, Jason Friedman, David Fritzinger, Ken Frydman, Masako Fukuoka, Cynthia Fulgham, Andrew Fuston

Harold Gainer, Daniela Galli, Robin Gannes, Gregory Galford, Sargent Gardiner, John Garrison, Lisa Garriss, Talia Gavish, Suzanne Gehlert, Franca Giammarino, John Ginocchio, Terry Gipson, Evan Goldman, Nicholas Gonsor, Michael Gonzaga, Keith Gonzalez, Mercedes Gonzalez, Anna Marie Grasso, Carolyn Green, Lori Greene, Scott Grodesky, Diego Gronda, Niels Guldager

Marc Hacker, Halla Haraldsdottir Hamar, Douglas Hamilton, Herve Hamon, Patrick Han, Eskild Hanson, Tracy Harrison, Jessica Hawkins, Fumiyo Hayashi, Allison Hecht, Molly Heintz, Josh Held, Phil Henshaw, Jeffrey Higgenbottom, Gabriella Caicedo Hillis, Fumio Hirakawa, Mary Homer, Bradley Horn, Stephen Horniak, Todd Hulin, Alice Hunt, Samantha Hunt, Cyrlene Hurley, Karen Hutchinson

Michael Iorii

David Jimeniz, Jason Johnson, Maia Johnson, Wade Johnson, Bock Duk Jueng, Istvan Juhasz, Eun Joo Jun

Afrim Kacaj, Mirveta Kacaj, Jung Yun Kang, Nora Kanter, Allison Karn, Hazel Karsten, David Katz, Leah Katz-Nelson, Christon Kellogg, Dana Kenn, Donald Keppler, Scott Kester, George Kewin, Khalida Khan, Sergei Khoroshilov, Ahkyeong Kim, Jee Won Kim, Jung-Jin Kim, Anastasia Kinsella, Anjna Kirpalani, Phillip Klinkon, Ivan Knapp, Lorraine Knapp, Patricia Knight, Jean Pierre Kocher-Kohn, Jahae Koo, Jefferson Koo, Shari Krasnow, John Krifka, Ann Krsul, Ping Ku, Mimi Kueh, David Kutos

Linda Lachick, Theresa Lagasse, Geraldine Lambert, Inna Lara, Vennie Lau, Linda Laucirica, Antonio Layco, Chin Lee, Don Lee, Edwin Lee, Katherine Lee, David Lefkowitz, Julie Leibeman, Steven Leone, Peggy Leung, Alex Li, Chih-hui Li Xintian, Stephen Liang Xintian, Lisa Lichtenberger, Jennifer Light, Digna Lima, Michael Linczyc, Robert Lipson, Gregory Lombardi, Agueda Lopez, Lisa Lorino, Claudine Luchsinger, Sarah Luhtala, Justin Lui, Dunn Lyman

Charlotte Macaux, Jaime Machado, Joan MacKeith, Kathleen MacKenzie, Waldo Maffei, Nancy Mah, Kavita Mallick, Maurizio Manzo, Eric Marcus, Teresa Mastropierro, Satako Matsuno, Evan Elizabeth McCauley, Mara McClelland, Aaron McDonald, Jesse McDougall, James McGovern, Norris McLeod, John Meder, Brian Mednick, Michael Meister, Jacqueline Melendez, Michael Mensch, Sean Meriwether, David Mexico, Yair Millet, Onjin Min, Myron Mirgorodsky, Kinnaresh Mistry, Kevin Mitchell, Mateo Mize, Paul Molina, James Monday, David Moore, Sean Morales, Brendan Moran, Christopher Morris, Jennifer Morris, Randy Morton, Kathleen Murphy, Mary Kate Murray, Nicholas Musolino

Linda Nagaoka, Carol Ann Nameck, Christopher Nelson, Claire Nelson, Anurag Nema, Cynthia Nemo, Katherine Newsom, Wai Ng, Doan-Trang Nguyen, Lia Nielson, Maja Nikolic, Timothy Nissen, Susan Norr

Laura O'Brien, Linda O'Brien, Peter O'Loghlen, David Ortega, Juan Dario Ortiz, Ulises Otero, Emilio Ozaeta

Karen Parada, Lee Parmenter, Vaishali Patel, Sarita Pawar, Sheela Pawar, Sergio Paz, Alix Pearlstein, Tomas Pedrasa, Thomas Pedrazzi, Christian Perez, Anthony Persaud, Miguel Petruscak, James Pertusi, Damion Phillips, Fredric Pichon, Benjamin Pietro Filardo, Nicole Pillorge, Robert Polacek, Paulette Polimeni, Christopher Pollard, Alexander Pomarico, Phillip Pond, Lisa Pope, Erica Pritchard, Allen Prusis

Bobby Rabinowitz, Steven Rahe, Nanette Rayman, Heather Rebhotz, Roque Rey, Barry Richards, Joseph Richvalsky, Tonya Rife, Charles Rittman, David Rockwell, Lisa Roberts, Robert Robinowitz, Antonio Rodriguez,

Ines Rodriguez, Nicholas Rodriguez, Olga Rodriguez, Howard Roman, Timothy Rooney, Ivan Rosa, Luis Andres Rosario, Deborah Rosado, Jayneb Rose, Thomas Rosenkilde, Alexander Ross, Sally Ross, Sandra Roten, Julia Roth, Nicholas Ruderman

Mark Safan, Germinia Salamone, Tom Salazar, Amber Sami, Lourdes Sanchez, Derek Sanders, Aracelis Santana, Steve Santillan, Eric Santini, Maral Sarizosen, Thomas Peter Sarr, Alejandro Sarria, David Schefer, Joanie Schlafer, Gary Schmidt, Eve-Lynn Schoenstein, Christine Scholtz, Ariela Schulman, James Scott, Michelle Segre, Robert Seidel, Nina Seirafi, Arezoo Shafizadeh, Elina Shchervinsky, Paul Shurtleff, Adele Sijuwade, David Silver, Michael Silver, Kimberly Silvia-Hall, Evelyn Simeoli, Manmeet Singh, Chris Smith, Nellie King Solomon, Paul Song, Mike Soriano, Kendra Lynne Sosothikul, Mary Spackman, John Spirou, Robert Stack, Brian Stackable, Gregory Stanford, Anna Starling, Steven Starr, Amy Statuto, Nina Stern, Joslin Grae Stewart, Gary Stluka, Shawn Sullivan, Joseph Sultana, Richard Summa, Michael Suomi

Kiwami Takao, Tomoko Tanaka, Kye-Jing Tan, Catherine Taylor, Adam Teitelbaum, Victoria Tentler, Steve Terr, Darren Teruel, Christopher Tetens, Stephanie Thacker, Katherine Tharp, Nancy Thiel, Karen Thomas, Louisa Thompson, Julia Thomson, Seaneen Thorpe, Dominic Tolson, Raymond Tom, Peter Tomashevski, Mamoudou Toure, Salvatore Tranchina, Kathleen Triem, Samuel Trimble, Richard Truemner, Robert Twardzik

Bruce Umbarger, Geoffrey Upton, Rachel Urkowitz

Gerald Valgora, Awa Valiente, John Van Aken, Carmen Vasquez, Paul Vega, Hillary Carlson Verni, Joseph Verni, Emanuelle Visconti, Eddy Viteri, Gerald K. Vyhmeister

Sanah Waheed, Jo Walker, James Wassell, Martin Weiner, Alan Weinstein, Charles Wermers, David Wermert, Paul Whiting, David Wilbourne, Sonia Garcia Willson, Lorrin Wong, Beata Wroblewski, Cameron Wu, Hiltrud Wuerz

Yuka Yamaoka, Sergei Yaralov, Wei Yeong, Alice Yiu, Milissa Yoon, Seong-Hye Yoon, Julie Yurasek

Alejandro Zaballero, Bettina Zerza

221

PERFORMING ART, CINEMA, AND ENTERTAINMENT

1995

Copperfield's Magic Underground*
New York, New York
Late Night Magic

Festival Disney Gate*
Paris, France
Walt Disney Imagineering

Minton's Jazz Club*
New York, New York
The Myriad Restaurant Group

New Amsterdam Rooftop Theatre*
New York, New York
Walt Disney Theatrical

1996

Battersea Power Station*
London, England
Victor Wong and Sheldon Gordon

Playdium
Toronto, Canada
Playdium Entertainment Corporation

Loews Theatres
New Brunswick, New Jersey
Loews Cineplex Entertainment

Loews Theatres, 84th Street
New York, New York
Loews Cineplex Entertainment

Magic Johnson Theatres
Atlanta, Georgia
Loews Cineplex Entertainment

1997

Gaumont Cinemas at Festival Disney
EuroDisney, France
EuroDisney/Gaumont Cinemas

Star Theatres
Southfield, Michigan
Star Theatres

Innoventions, Tomorrow Land, Disneyland*
Los Angeles, California
Walt Disney Imagineering

Loews Theatres, Keystone Park
Dallas, Texas
Loews Cineplex Entertainment

1999

Cirque du Soleil
Orlando, Florida
Walt Disney Imagineering/
Cirque du Soleil

Loews 42nd Street Theatres
New York, New York
Loews Cineplex Entertainment

Star Theatres, Great Lakes Crossing Mall
Auburn Hills, Missouri
Star Theatres

Loews Theatres
Methuen, Massachusetts
Loews Cineplex Entertainment

Sony Theatres—Metreon
San Francisco, California
Loews Cineplex Entertainment

TKTS Competition*
New York, New York
Van Alen Institute

Corlears Hook Pavilion Amphitheatre (proposed)
New York, New York
The Pavilion Group

2000

Proposed Broadway Theater*
MGM Grand Hotel,
Las Vegas, Nevada
MGM Grand Hotel, Inc.

2001

The IMAX at Rio Casino*
Las Vegas, Nevada
Gaylord Entertainment

Kodak Theatre
Hollywood, California
TrizecHahn Development

Loews Boston Millennium
Boston, Massachusetts
Millennium Partners

SET DESIGN

2001–2002

The Rocky Horror Show
New York, New York
Jordan Roth Productions

2002

Hairspray
Seattle, Washington, and
New York, New York
Margo Lion Ltd.

HOSPITALITY

1996

Loews Regency Hotel Library Lounge
New York, New York
Loews Hotels

1998

W New York
New York, New York,
Starwood Hotels and Resorts
Worldwide, Inc.

Away Spa at W New York
New York, New York
Starwood Hotels and Resorts
Worldwide, Inc.

2000

Equinox
New York, New York
Bell Development

W Union Square
New York, New York
The Related Companies/Starwood
Hotels and Resorts Worldwide, Inc.

2001

Chambers
New York, New York
Ira Drukier/Richard Born/Steve Caspi

2002

Mohegan Sun, Casino of the
Sky, Hotel Lobby
Uncasville, Connecticut
Mohegan Tribal Gaming
Authority/Sun International

Watercolor Inn
Watercolor, Florida
The St. Joe Company

2003

The Diegan
San Diego, California
Diegan, LLC

2004

Art'otel
London, England
The Red Sea Group

HEALTH CARE

2001

Children's Hospital at Montefiore
Bronx, New York
Montefiore Medical Center

CASINOS

1994

Forum Phase III*
Las Vegas, Nevada
Gordan Brandt

1996–2002

Mohegan Sun, Casino of the
Earth and Casino of the Sky
Uncasville, Connecticut
Mohegan Tribal Gaming
Authority/Sun International

1996

ITT/Planet Hollywood Casino & Hotel*
Las Vegas, Nevada
ITT Sheraton

1998

Alladin Music Project
Las Vegas, Nevada
Alladin Gaming LLC

OFFICES

1995

@Radical Media Offices
New York, New York
@Radical Media

1997

@Radical Media Offices
Santa Monica, California
@Radical Media

2002

McCann-Erickson Offices
New York, New York
McCann-Erickson

2003

Foote Cone Belding Offices
New York, New York
Foote Cone Belding

SPORTS ARCHITECTURE

1997

Coca-Cola Skyfield, Turner Field
Atlanta, Georgia
The Coca-Cola Company

Coca-Cola @ Stade de France*
Paris, France
The Coca-Cola Company

1998

National Football League, The Hacienda*
Carson, California
Michael Ovitz/NFL

1999

*National Football League, Coliseum at Exposition Park***
Los Angeles, California
Michael Ovitz/NFL

2000

Comerica Park, Detroit Master Plan and Tigers Ball Park
Detroit, Michigan
Olympia Development

Fantasy Sports Complex (proposed)
New York, New York

Minute Maid "Squeeze Play" at Enron Field
Houston, Texas
The Coca-Cola Company

2001

Pittsburgh Steelers, Steelers Stadium
Pittsburgh, Pennsylvania
Pittsburgh Steelers

AIRPORTS

2001

Las Vegas Airport (proposed)
Las Vegas, Nevada
McCarran International Airport and
the Clark County Board of
Commissioners

Singapore Airport Terminal 2 (proposed)
Singapore
Civil Aviation Authority of Singapore

RETAIL

1994–1998

Morgenthal-Frederics Opticians
New York, New York
Rick Morgenthal

1995

CBS Retail Store
New York, New York
CBS

1996

Best Cellars
Nationwide
Joshua Wesson/Richard Marmet

Victoria Ward Fashion Mall*
Honolulu, Hawaii
The Gordon Company

1999

Jersey Gardens
Elizabeth, New Jersey
Glimcher Properties

Prudential Retail
Bedminster, New Jersey,
and Coral Gables, Florida
Prudential Insurance Company of
America

2000

Sultan's Garden Palace in the Desert Passage at Aladdin
Las Vegas, Nevada
TrizecHahn Development

2001

Discover Mills
Atlanta, Georgia
The Mills Corporation

LaLalounis Jewelry Store
New York, New York
Demetra LaLalounis

2002

Crayola
Arundel Mills, Maryland
Binney & Smith

Origins
New York, New York
Origins/Estee Lauder

2004

Jordan's Furniture
Reading, Massachusetts
Jordan's Furniture

MASTER PLANNING

1996

Detroit Master Plan*
Detroit, Michigan
Olympia Development

1997

Downtown Disney's The West Side
Walt Disney World, Florida
The Walt Disney Company

1999–2001

Madison Square Garden Entertainment District*
New York, New York
Vornado Realty Trust

2001

Bronx Zoo
Bronx, New York
Wildlife Conservation Society

Complexe Cirque
Hong Kong, China
Cirque du Soleil

Steelers Village
Pittsburgh, Pennsylvania
Pittsburgh Steelers

2002

Pier Park Drive
Panama City Beach, Florida
The St. Joe Company

Disney Village Master Plan
Paris, France
The Walt Disney Company

PUBLIC WORKS

2001–2002

World Trade Center Platform
New York, New York
Office of the Mayor, New York City

RESIDENTIAL

1994

Tribeca Tower
New York, New York,
The Related Companies

1998

Union Square South
New York, New York
The Related Companies

1999

Sagamore
New York, New York
The Related Companies

Sassa Residence
New York, New York
Ellen and Scott Sassa

2001

The Sonoma
New York, New York
The Related Companies

Bridgetower
New York, New York
The Brodsky Organization

The Lyric
New York, New York
The Related Companies

2002

Murano Grande
Miami, Florida
The Related Group of Florida

West 23rd Street
New York, New York
The Related Companies

2003

455 Central Park West
New York, New York
MCL Companies

RESTAURANTS

1992

Vong
New York, New York
Jean-Georges Vongerichten/Lettuce
Entertain You Enterprises

1993

Christers**
New York, New York
Christer Larsson

1994

Nobu
New York, New York
The Myriad Restaurant Group

1995

Planet Hollywood
Orlando, Florida
Planet Hollywood International, Inc.

The Monkey Bar
New York, New York
The Glazier Group

Baang
Greenwich, Connecticut
Signature Entertainment

Tapika
New York, New York
The Glazier Group

1996

Loews Regency Library
New York, New York
Loews Corporation

Lipstick Café
New York, New York
Giraldi-Suarez

1997

Official All Star Café
New York, New York
Planet Hollywood International, Inc.

Payard Patisserie & Bistro
New York, New York
Daniel Boulud/François Payard

Rainbow Room*
New York, New York
David Emil, BEN Partners

1998

Animator's Palate
Disney Magic
Disney Cruise Line

Café Milan
London, England
Showtime Restaurants

**Grand Central Terminal
Dining Concourse**
New York, New York
Grand Central Station, Metropolitan
Transportation Authority

Lidia's
Kansas City, Missouri
Lidia's Restaurant Group

Next Door Nobu
New York, New York
The Myriad Restaurant Group

Saks Espresso and Juice Bar
Houston, Texas
Saks Fifth Avenue

1999

Animator's Palate
Disney Wonder
Disney Cruise Line

Michael Jordan's The Steak
House N.Y.C.
New York, New York
The Glazier Group

Nobu
Las Vegas, Nevada
The Myriad Restaurant Group

Ruby Foo's Dim Sum
and Sushi Palace
New York, New York
B. R. Guest

Vong
Chicago, Illinois
Jean-Georges Vongerichten/Lettuce
Entertain You Enterprises

2000

Big Bowl Restaurant
Chicago, Illinois
Lettuce Entertain You Enterprises

Bongos
Miami, Florida
Emilio Estefan/Jay Cross

District
New York, New York
The Muse Hotel

Joe's Stone Crab
Chicago, Illinois
Lettuce Entertain You Enterprises

King Fish
Boston, Massachusetts
The Olive Group

Luca, Boca Raton Resort and Club
Boca Raton, Florida
Boca Raton Resort

Rosa Mexicano
New York, New York
Shelter Ruppert Management

Strip House
New York, New York
The Glazier Group

2001

Alma de Cuba
Philadelphia, Pennsylvania
Starr Restaurants LLC

Bar Avion, JFK Airport
New York, New York
Restaurant Associates

Citarella
New York, New York
Citarella

Delancey's Bar, JFK Airport
New York, New York
Restaurant Associates

Emeril's
New Orleans, Louisiana
Emeril's Homebase

Lidia's
Pittsburgh, Pennsylvania
Lidia's Restaurant Group

Little Buddha
Las Vegas, Nevada
Raymond Visan, George V.
Restauration

Olive's W Union Square
New York, New York
The Olive Group

Pod
Philadelphia, Pennsylvania
Starr Restaurants LLC

Town
New York, New York
Town Restaurant, LLC

Tuscany, Mohegan Sun
Uncasville, Connecticut
The Olive Group

2002

Buddha Bar
New York, New York
Raymond Visan, George V.
Restauration

Django
New York, New York
Main Street Restaurant Partners

Geisha
New York, New York
Thompson & Sears, LLC

Fish Out of Water
Watercolor, Florida
The St. Joe Company

Lidia's
Salt Lake City, Utah
Lidia's Restaurant Group

Roppongi Hills Restaurant
Roppongi Hills, Tokyo
Soho's Hospitality Group Co., Ltd.

Tchoup Chop
Orlando, Florida
Emeril's Homebase

CLUBS/BARS

1990

Tatou Restaurant and Club**
New York, New York
Mark Fleischman

1991

**Le Bar Bat Restaurant
& Nightclub****
New York, New York
Minerva West Incorporation

1992

Tatou Restaurant and Club**
Beverly Hills, California
Mark Fleischman

1997

Roseland
New York, New York
Roseland

1998

Whiskey Blue at W New York
New York, New York
Midnight Oil

2000

Underbar at W Union Square
New York, New York
Midnight Oil

EVENTS

1994

DIFFA/Metropolitan Home Street
of Shops, Library for Jeremy Irons
New York, New York
DIFFA/Metropolitan Home

1998

DIFFA Dining by Design,
The Secret Garden
New York, New York
DIFFA

1999

DIFFA Dining by Design,
I Get a Kick from Champagne
New York, New York
DIFFA/Champagne Mumm

2000

DIFFA, The Great Bazaar
New York, New York
DIFFA

DIFFA/Steuben Celebration by Design
New York, New York
DIFFA/Steuben

EXHIBITION AND TELEVISION
SET DESIGN

1996

**I.D. Magazine Annual Design
Awards Exhibition**
New York, New York
I.D. Magazine

**Television Food Network
"Dining for Two"**
New York, New York
Television Food Network

1997

I.D. Magazine Annual Design
Awards Exhibition
New York, New York
I.D. Magazine

"Union Square" Television Show Set
Directed by Jim Burroughs
NBC

Chef Studio (proposed)
New York, New York

2002

Declaration of Independence Road Trip
Winter Olympics
Salt Lake City, Utah
Norman Lear

*denotes unbuilt

** denotes designed by
Haverson/Rockwell Architecture

Projects appearing in italics are
represented in the book.

ACKNOWLEDGMENTS

I have many people to thank, but my deepest gratitude is reserved for everyone at Rockwell Group. The spirit and energy of this team has created an environment that is continuously challenging and engaging. Throughout the seventeen years of work that this book covers, a remarkable number of talented, brilliant, and on many occasions eccentric people have participated in the creative process. I thank all of them for sharing their ideas and for listening to mine, cogent or not!

A few people at Rockwell Group have been particularly instrumental in creating this book. A special thanks goes to Marc Hacker. He is the guiding force behind this project and I would never have been able to even think about doing it without him. Barry Richards has been a joyful and intrepid contributor on this and many other projects. And without the indefatigable Joan MacKeith and Kate Newsom, this project simply would not have been delivered to the printer.

I am lucky to have found Richard Olsen. He has championed this book from the beginning and I am grateful for his editorial guidance and leadership. The editorial staff at Universe, Christopher Steighner and Charles Miers, has been constantly supportive in bringing this publication to fruition. Thanks to Sheryl Shade for getting the ball rolling and to Chee Pearlman for her savvy and sure-handed editorial advice. John Klotnia at Opto Design has worked tirelessly to make the design of this book more than I could ever have imagined, and the photo research talents of Kevin Kwan have been indispensable.

I am deeply indebted to every one of the stellar writers who contributed their insights into what we do. Their views allow us to step back from the fray and to understand our own process more critically. A special thank you to Henry Edwards for his friendship, guidance, and patience.

There are three people to whom this book is dedicated: Marcia, Sammy, and Lola. You are the center of my world.

—David Rockwell

BASELINE CAPTIONS

INTRODUCTION

Rockwell Group office

NOBU

Octopus Tiradito, Nobu Style • One Man Dining • Nori • Plan • *Apartment Project, "Slip in Tokorozawa,"* Kita-Urakucho, Tokorozawa, Japan, 1983, Tadashi Kawamata • *Primitive Hut* • Birch • Astroboy • Bamboo grove • Chinatown fish • Kabuki theater play—*Yasuna's Mad Scene*

VONG

Lipstick • Thai newspaper collage • Sunset on Wat Mahathat • *Childs Restaurant, 1899* • Plaid patterns • David Rockwell in *The King and I*

POD

Sleepers, Woody Allen • Construction mesh • TWA Building, JFK Airport • *2001: A Space Odyssey*, Stanley Kubrick • Pod product box • Rubber-dipped flatware and glassware • Plan • Sketch

RUBY FOO'S DIM SUM AND SUSHI PALACE

San Francisco restaurant • Mah-jongg game • Postcard • Mah-jongg pieces • Neon streetscape • Gloria Swanson in *Sunset Boulevard*, Billy Wilder • Three Asian ladies

MICHAEL JORDAN'S THE STEAK HOUSE N.Y.C.

Grand Central Terminal • *North by Northwest*, Alfred Hitchcock • Electrolux Model 30 • Trains, from *The Twentieth Century Limited, 1938–1967* • Michael Jordan • *North by Northwest*, Alfred Hitchcock

ROSA MEXICANO

Mexican dresses • Acapulco cliff diver • Bullfight programs • Girl in seatbelt • Petals • Tehuantepec, Mexico objects • Pants on a clothesline • *Barragán House* (Tacubaya, Mexico City), 1947, Luis Barragán

ANIMATOR'S PALATE

Back Somersault, sequence taken from *The Attitudes of Animals in Motion*, Eadweard Muybridge • Model of a ship • *Pleasantville*, Gary Ross

CHAMBERS

Alexander Calder in his studio, 1941 • Pipes • *Who Am We*, Do-ho Suh • Four Seasons restaurant • Paley Park • Chandelier collage • *Untitled, 1998*, Mark Keffer • Furry fabric • *King Kong*, Merian C. Cooper and Ernest B. Schoedsack • *Pastoral Paradise*, John Newsom

W NEW YORK

The Secret Garden, illustrated by Graham Rust • Oasis, Libya • Forest; Chichibu, Japan • Fire • Water • Canyon • Laurentian Library entry stairs • *Cockatoo and Corks*, Joseph Cornell • Whiskey Blue sign • Wheatgrass

W UNION SQUARE

Corsets • *Edward Scissorhands*, Tim Burton • Guardian sign • Topiary • Gerber daisies

CHILDREN'S HOSPITAL AT MONTEFIORE

Foucault pendulum, Tom Otterness • Planets • Girl with microscope • Boy with viewfinder • Explorer's Kit

BEST CELLARS

That Touch of Mink, Delbert Mann • Best Cellars graphics • Dots candy box • Wine rack • Automat

MORGENTHAL-FREDERICS

Jacqueline Onassis stops over in Rome en route to Greece • Dovetail joint • Shaker chairs • Shakers' dance

JERSEY GARDENS

Treehouse • Crystal Palace • Grass in the sidewalk • Chain link

THE GREAT BAZAAR

Invitation • Moussine copper merchants in the old bazaar • Moulay Ismael Mausoleum • Great Bazaar Lantern • Rajasthan, Pushkar fair • Cindy Crawford's Pillow

A LIBRARY FOR JEREMY IRONS

Iconic tree • Jeremy Irons, *Brideshead Revisited*, Michael Lindsay-Hogg and Charles Sturridge • Books • Japanese script • Handwritten Yeats's text

THE SECRET GARDEN, I GET A KICK FROM CHAMPAGNE

A Mad Tea-Party, Charles Lutwidge Dodgson • Nest • Bubbles • Crocus drawing • Glass beads

I.D. EXHIBIT

Orary • *Ming the Merciless* comic • I.D. Logo

PRODUCTS

Interior of Madame Curie's laboratory

CIRQUE DU SOLEIL

Theater at Delphi • Spider web • *Under the Big Top* • Rooster • *Gas Tank (Telescoping Type), off Pulaski Bridge*, Jersey City, New Jersey, U.S.A., 1981, 1989, Bernd and Hilla Becher • Cirque performers, *La Nouba* • Big tent

COMPLEXE CIRQUE

Urban carpet concept • Renderings

KODAK THEATRE

Cleopatra, Joseph L. Mankiewicz • Grauman's theater • Opéra Garnier, Paris • *Gold Diggers*, 1933, Mervyn LeRoy • Cher

THE ROCKY HORROR SHOW

Curse of Frankenstein, Terence Fisher • *The Pont Neuf Wrapped*, Paris, 1975–85, Christo and Jeanne-Claude • Laboratory sketches • Cod. Atl., fol. 24r, *Automatic file-making machine*, Leonardo da Vinci

HAIRSPRAY

Necco Wafer–inspired background pattern • Lite Brite wall • Form stone • *Hairspray*, John Waters • Dick Clark and Connie Stevens on *American Bandstand*

COCA-COLA SKYFIELD, TURNER FIELD

Adirondack chairs • Jackie Robinson • Watts Towers • Coke Ad, 1990 • *Boys at Play*

COMERICA PARK

Bat • The Detroit Institute of Arts • *Batcolumn, 1977*, Claes Oldenburg and Coosje van Bruggen, Harold Washington Social Security Center, 600 West Madison Street, Chicago, 96 ft. 8 in. (h) x 9 ft. 9 in. (d) on base 4 ft. (h) x 10 ft. (d) • Ebbets Field • Bronx Zoo elephant sculpture

FANTASY SPORTS COMPLEX

Football • Puck • Basketball

MOHEGAN SUN, CASINO OF THE EARTH

Two skins • Casino of the Earth plan • Mohegan basket • Leaves • Stone • Grand Canyon • Sketches • Cecil B. DeMille

MOHEGAN SUN, CASINO OF THE SKY

Casino of the Earth and Sky plan • *Lonepine*, Deborah Butterfield • Park Guell • *Ocean 5*, Piet Mondrian • Wombi Rock • *The Rink*, A. J. Antoon

AFTERWORD

David Rockwell • World Trade Center Viewing Platform: Following the attack on the World Trade Center, David Rockwell, Kevin Kennon, Elizabeth Diller and Ricardo Scofidio collaborated to design and build a public viewing platform at ground zero in response to growing public demand and at the request of New York City. They worked with more than one hundred volunteers in the municipal and the private domain to have the platform completed by December 30, 2001. The group established a not-for-profit organization, W.T.C. Platform Foundation Inc., to raise money for the construction.